Pouring Ketchup

HURT Stories Between HOPE.

Dennis Cook

WestBow
PRESS
A DIVISION OF THOMAS NELSON

ISBN: 978-1-4497-6646-7 (e)
ISBN: 978-1-4497-6647-4 (sc)
ISBN: 978-1-4497-6648-1 (hc)

WestBow Press books may be ordered through booksellers or by contacting:

WestBow Press
A Division of Thomas Nelson
1663 Liberty Drive
Bloomington, IN 47403
www.westbowpress.com
1-(866) 928-1240

Library of Congress Control Number: 2012916635

Printed in the United States of America

WestBow Press rev. date: 9/17/2012

Contents

Endorsments:

"Dennis Cook is one of the most creative people I know. He has an incredible ability to communicate the truths contained in God's word through the use of powerful stories. His stories have not only challenged my thinking over the years, but they have stirred my heart to want to become more like Jesus and less like a Pharisee."

Jim Wood (A college buddy I barrowed notes from)

Dennis has a way of telling a story that inspires me to want to write a few lines of hope in those around me.

Matt Miller (A friend I eat barbeque wings with)

These stories remind me that no matter how alone I may feel, I am not. Sometimes we think we are so different and these stories prove were not. Hurt doesn't have to be the final answer, just part of the journey.

Michelle Ernst (A Mom)

These stories are practical and provoking at the same time. I see myself in each situation and at times don't like how I would respond. Dennis's creative approach will pull you in and make you think about the way we daily interact with people. I strongly recommend this book, it is easy to read and yet challenging!
Mick Veach (A friend who showed me what real faith looked like)

I am a slow reader but the way Dennis writes makes me want to sprint to the end. He is very transparent and doesn't use a lot of fancy words. As I read through these stories I've learned more about him in the last year that the eighteen years I have known him. Thanks for letting me in the back room of your life.

Darrin Koester (A good friend from back in the day who is a story-holic)

Dedication

Heidi, Mackenzie, and Morgan thanks for always believing in me and granting me eternal dibs on the remote.

To Don!

Forward:

Everyone has a story, and even if the story is told it is seldom heard. Gone is the art of listening in today's sound-bite world. The attention span of a hearer is taken in by just bits and bytes, tweets and twitters. Dennis Cook is an artist, a master listener and the page is his canvas for pen, ink, and the words of your portrait. The art of listening comes alive in his observations of real life. You can find yourself in any one of Dennis's stories, if not today, then, the next time you read it you'll be there. This is a book that you will read and re-read, laughing one moment and crying the next. Like life itself

Ron Slager (A great friend who treats me like I'm part of his family)

Thanks for All. You Have Done To Being Me Along In my Walk For Over 30 years

Acknowledgements:

Thanks to my wife Heidi who always believed I could write this goofy book even when my fears and doubts prophesized I couldn't. Every time I pitched my "pen" in the trash saying "I quit!" you always dove in and rescued it and put it back in my hand. Your steady encouragement will be rewarded with a life time supply of chocolate and the use of the remote on Tuesday's and Thursday's.

Thanks Mackenzie and Morgan, my two teenage daughters, who always seem to know when I need a pep talk or the truth.

Mackenzie, your simple prayer when I struggled to start this book was amazing. When I let my past darkness almost keep me from writing you prayed "Dear God, help Dad know that you were always in his story even if he couldn't see you. You could see him and were holding his hand." I'm not sure if I bought what you were selling at the time but after writing this you were right. Your reward will be a full case of green and red Nerds and a new Jeep. Well at least one of the two.

Morgan, I don't know anybody who is more kind and can still just tell it like it is. When I was whining to you about what to do with some of the people who will hate Pouring Ketchup you said "Dad you don't write a book to the people who hate it you write it to the people who need it." Now stop whining and write your book." The good news is your reward will be what you have been begging for, an I Pad. The bad news is by the time I can afford one they will be sitting on dusty shelves at the Goodwill right next to the 8-Track Tapes. (I know, ask your mother what those are.)

Thanks to my parents and brother and sisters who have loved me through all the snags of life. Your reward will be in heaven some day. Sorry, I'm running out of cash with all this chocolate, candy and I Pad stuff.

Thanks to our church The Restoration Station for always letting me be me. You always believed in me even when I didn't. Your reward will be you are stuck with me and dounut holes each Sunday morning.

Thanks to all the people over the years after babbling out story after story said, "Dennis you should write a book someday." Well that someday is now and you better cough up a little cash and buy a few copies or I will find you. Your reward is I will no longer weary you with all my stories. You can now just buy the book.

Thanks to Ron and Jo for letting me write in your cozy basement and feeding me endless slabs of Ribs. Your house has always been a safe place to drop in when life falls apart. Your reward will be when I write my next book I will come and eat more Ribs with you both, with Ketchup.

Thanks to Michelle for all the hours you spent pouring over my manuscript trying to bring a little magic to my mess. Your reward will be sleep at nights.

Thanks to you for taking time to read a few stories from Pouring Ketchup. Your reward, I pray at the end of this book that you will feel a little closer to Hope than Hurt.

Introduction

What if people really knew who we were? When hurt imposes its crabby will on our lives, many of us lock up the scars in our private journals. We write down stuff for our eyes only. It's a safe place to hide our fears, failures, and frustrations with our self, our friends, and even God. Journals are never meant to be read to the world because if we read them publicly, they would reveal who we really are, what we really think, and how we really feel, and nobody wants to undress their soul in front of others to be made fun of, me included.

Somewhere behind the hallelujahs, the praise the Lords, and the God is good stuff is this real place only our journals have enough grace to accept. It's a place where one plus one doesn't equal two. It's a place where you mix red and blue and get grey, lots and lots of grey. It's a place where you're mad at God and feel He's mad at you. That's what journals hold, the stories of our lives; not the way we always want them, but the way they really are.

When God invited me to write a book exposing my own journal to the world, I politely rejected Him. Okay, not real politely. I told Him, *There's no way I'm ever going to reveal what I spent a lifetime concealing. God, I'm a pastor, and some of these stories don't make me look good, and as You know, a few don't even make me look like a Christian. So how about You and I make a deal? In my forty-seventh book I'll let the world snoop around in my journal, but not my first.*

I refused to hand over the key to my journal, knowing God would just blab it to the whole world. I was not going to write a book that makes me look way more human than holy.

That all changed one day when four—no, five—strangers walked into McDonald's, four adults by age only and a plump lady chaperone. You could see the four had gotten shortchanged on some of the things you and I take for granted each day. Being a bit bored, I watched their every move. The four could do virtually nothing by themselves. One of the guys was trying to pour ketchup, and let's just say he got it everywhere but in the tiny white paper cup. (More about that in chapter 1.)

As I eavesdroped on their flaws, failures, and frustrations, I realized these beautiful people had no "journals" in which to hide who they really were. Every day this quartet of folks lived out their fragile lives totally exposed to a world that talks more about them than to them.

It was as if God were saying, *I want you to write like these people live every day, an open journal to the world.* The stories you are about to read have been suffocating in beige pages between the covers of my leather journal for years. I am no longer forcing them to plug their noses and hold their breath. With much fear and trembling I'm inviting you into the pages of my life. Being truthful, I am very scared of what people will think of some of my less-than-flattering entries. For me it is easier just to fake it in public and take my chances with my journal.

I dedicate *Pouring Ketchup* to an amazing cast of characters you will shortly meet. Many of them are not—how would you put it—churchgoin' folks. Some would admit their halos are in the shop for repairs . Some have been sucker punched by lives they had not signed and up for. Some are standing on the edge, wondering that if there indeed is a God, *now* would be a good time for Him to show up. Some find life a bit more difficult than Sunday morning sermons make it sound. Some are rotting from the inside out because they can't forgive themselves or others. But most of all I dedicate *Pouring Ketchup* to four strangers who let me read a few pages of their open journals without fear of what I would find.

What would it be like if we let people know who we really are? What would it be like if we shared a few of our entries between hurt and hope? I pray you will find hope in your own story as you read about others looking for it in theirs.

All the stories in this book are true. Some are a composite with a few of the details and names changed and others are told without change.

Photo by Morgan Cook

1
Pouring Ketchup

I was sitting in a booth at a McDonald's in Kalamazoo, Michigan, trying to slop a little black ink on a white page for a book I was working on. I had a severe case of writer's block. It was so frustrating to have over fifty years of life under my belt and yet feel I had nothing important to share with the world. I had thoroughly grazed through the card catalog of my past trying to think of something clever to pass on but with no luck. I felt like I had all this profound stuff jammed inside me but didn't know how to get it out. I didn't want to write just to write. I started out to write this book not because I wanted to say something but rather because I had something to say.

The thought quietly kept tumbling through my mind: Dennis, if you had the microphone and could tell the whole world one thing, what would it be? It was an interesting question, but still no answer. That morning I'd occupied a booth for two-and-a-half hours and twenty-seven Cokes. I was kind of whining to God, Hey, I'm here to write this book You asked me to write, but you've got to kick in a few paragraphs. There was nothing from heaven falling on my booth or my book. So I patiently stayed cemented in my borrowed office just watching people.

After a few minutes of this public-surveillance thing a plump, middle-aged, African American lady walked in chaperoning four white people all of whom, you could just tell, had been dealt a less-than-winning hand in life. They would be considered adults by age only. The four giggled and poked each other as if at a junior high dance. Their clothes were as outdated as their hairstyles, but they sure were glad to be dining at McDonald's.

My eyes were spying on their every move. One of the men was trying to pour ketchup in one of those small, white, paper cups. He kept pumping the button but always missed the cup, and ketchup flopped everywhere. Another lady was trying to put a lid on her Coke but couldn't figure out what size. Another one kept missing her mouth as she tried to eat her salad. Her face had ranch dressing all over it. One man just kept rocking back and forth, smiling and grunting out more sounds than sentences that only he seemed to understand. After what seemed like four hours of fumbling around trying to eat meals any one of which would have taken me five minutes to inhale, they were almost done.

I began to imagine how different our lives were. I could pour ketchup, pick lids, and hit my mouth 99 percent of the time. I could order my own food. I could go to the bathroom by myself. I could dress myself and tie my own shoes. Yet all these things were uphill struggles every day of their lives. My life seemed so different from theirs. Who makes the call when people are born that this one will be able to pour ketchup but that one won't? That this one will be able to eat and that one will have to be fed? Though our two booths were only inches away, it seemed like the Grand Canyon separated our lives. I felt a little guilty for feeling so blessed.

Then I sensed God nudge me to do something that completely surprised me. He said, Ask them what they would say to the whole world if they had the microphone.

Whoa, God! Weren't you paying attention? Didn't You see what I saw?

It just seemed odd to ask people who couldn't pour ketchup or find the right lid what they would say to the whole world. But I was desperate, so I got out of the booth and took the three-inch walk.

I politely introduced myself to the woman in charge. She was wearing a jet-black T-shirt with red and silver sequins that boldly spelled out just one word "Love." It was a shirt that fit better in Vegas than in McDonald's, but oh, well. I explained to her I was writing a book and asked if I could please ask her one question. She cautiously agreed.

"If you had the 'microphone' and could tell the whole world one thing, what would it be?"

She slowly shifted her head toward the direction of her flock. I followed her eyes to her "sheep." I could tell we were looking at the same thing but seeing it totally differently. Some people have the gift of displaying compassion without saying a word. This woman had the gift of love written all over her silent stare.

After a few seconds her eyes moistened, and she spoke with the compassion of a veteran saint. Without looking at me she said, "I would tell the whole world to treat other people the way you wanted to be treated. It doesn't matter if you're red, yellow, black, or white."

I wasn't sure if she had stolen that from the Bible or learned it on the streets; no doubt she had been forced to witness countless rude stares and comments aimed at defenseless folks who wear ranch dressing like makeup. No doubt she had been wounded by careless comments about color aimed at her. But I guess it didn't matter where she had gotten it because it was evident she "got it." I praised her.

"Wow! That comes right from the Bible." She refused the halo and didn't care where "it" had come from as long as "it" made it to her four folks.

As I was walking away, assuming my assignment was over, God repeated, I told you to ask the four what they would say to the world if they had the mic.

But God, I don't think they will get the depth of Your philosophical question. Almost on cue, while I was informing God about what people do and don't get, they each gave me their one sentence.

"Hey, mister, it's cold out today."

"Do you have a warm coat?"

"Oh, I don't like the cold."

"Do you like the cold?"

I played along, smiling and pretending to shiver, saying, "No, I don't like the cold either." Then one lady's face lit up with a smile as big as her ranch-covered cheeks would allow. She said something I won't soon forget: "Hey, mister, you're just like us. We don't like the cold and you don't like the cold, so that makes you just like us."

That sentence caught me off-guard. I didn't know what to say. I don't think I ever would have used my one sentence to the whole world to say they were like me, yet they had used theirs to say I was like them. It was so weird; I had just spent the previous hour thinking I was nothing like them. I could pour my own ketchup and select my own lid. I didn't miss my mouth most of the time, and I seldom wore ranch dressing like lipstick. I had not been thinking I was better, just different.

Without warning, a boulder from heaven came crashing down on my false perception. God relayed, You're just like them, Dennis. You think because you can pour ketchup, pick the right lid, and shovel food in your mouth you don't need Me. Oh, you'll call on Me when you get low on cash or need a parking spot or when the flames get too high or hot. You'll whine and complain when you get writers' block, thinking I'm holding back on you. But most of the time you go about your life doing your own thing your own way.

That hurt my feelings, not because God was wrong but because He was right. I did tell Him to leave me alone at times. I was a big boy who could

3

get my own lids, feed myself, and pour my own ketchup. Then, like always, my life would fall apart, and lids, ranch dressing, and ketchup would explode everywhere. Embarrassed, I'd cry out for help. God, please help me clean up this mess I made of my life again.

God seldom answered me when and how I would like, but He does answer. That morning I had been whining and complaining about not having anything clever to share with the world. So what did God do? He ushered in four angels dressed in outdated clothes and hair led by a plump saint in a black T-shirt with heaven's logo bedazzled all over it. I finally realized it was the kind of shirt that fit better in McDonald's than in Vegas.

Dennis, I sent these people to you this morning to illustrate to you how much you need me even if you can pour ketchup. They know every day they can't get dressed, can't cook, can't drive, or tie their own shoes without help. The advantage these four have over you is they know they can't pour ketchup.

What a great surprise I received at McDonald's that morning. God kicked in way more than a few paragraphs. He sent me the whole story; not mine, but theirs. Those four fragile angels and the saint shuffled out the way they shuffled in, giggling and poking. I was sad, feeling like God had somehow just left McDonald's.

They all supplied me with enough ink to slop over the whole world with two simple thoughts: Treat other people the way you wanted to be treated whether they are red, yellow, black or white. And admit at times we all need a little help pouring ketchup.

2

Stained Glass

I was attending a weeklong conference in Atlanta to help pastors be better pastors. I was surrounded by the saints of the past 2,000 years immortalized in stained glass. I thought the church was one of the nicest buildings I had ever been in. The front of the church was draped with a million-dollar pipe organ that would barely fit into Noah's ark. The floors were imported marble, so clean we could have served lunch on them. The Gothic gold chandeliers hanging over our heads were casting a warm light able to melt even the grumpiest heart. I had a hunch they didn't come from Walmart. The pews were padded and gift wrapped in royal red velour. Scented candles flickered in the front of the church and flooded the room with a heavenly aroma. This place was so heavenly minded that the bathrooms were stocked with Angel Soft toilet paper. I didn't know what heaven looked like, but this joint had to be close.

When I got there I was fired up to get fired up. From 8 a.m. till 10 p.m. there was nothing but sermons, sermons, and more sermons. It's hard for some people to stay awake for an hour on Sunday morning, but we were sitting through eight of them. I learned that just because you're a pastor you aren't disqualified from stealing a few z's between the amens and the hallelujahs. Sometimes to pass the time during a less-than-stirring sermon I counted all the people sleeping in the room.

Well, on day four of five, what had started out as a spiritual sprint was slowing down to a lethargic limp. My once-fired-up faith was starting to fizzle. I hoped my confession would not draw lightning from heaven, but I was bored out of my mind. I didn't think I could swallow another sermon or soak up another spiritual trick to obligate God to do what we want when we want. I didn't think I could gulp down one more preacher trying to convince me that all my problems could be solved if I simply bought their book. I thought inhaling any more sermons would spin me into a spiritual coma.

Guilty thoughts swarmed around me like Michigan mosquitoes. Dennis, you're a pastor; you shouldn't feel this way. Dennis, there are millions of people in the world who have never heard even one sermon. Guilt reminded me of what I had reminded so many others: "You can never get too much Jesus." I didn't want to argue or justify my guilt any longer, so I gave myself permission to slip out of the sermon-athon.

I walked outside and sat on the church steps absorbing Atlanta's number-one tourist attraction, the sun. I rolled up my sleeves to get an early start on a farmer's tan. I used the five cement steps for a recliner, closed my eyes, and pretended to be at a beach. I'm not sure if I dozed off or just wished I had. All I know is when I woke up, a black woman was sitting two feet from me, watching me drool.

I asked her name, and she twirled her head away from me, signaling keep out. As I was one, a bit nosey, and two, bored and doing anything to delay going back into the preachers' paradise, I asked again, "What's your name?" Once again she ignored me with her silence. I decided I was not going to barge in beyond her barrier, so I resumed my position on my concrete recliner.

After a few minutes of silence she asked in a Southern drawl, "Excuse me, do you go to this place? And by the way, my name's Patty."

I leaned up and replied, "No, Patty, I'm just here for a pastors' conference."

"Oh, you're a pastor," she said as though she felt sorry for me. "Then why aren't you on the inside with the other pastors?"

I smiled thinking, Hey, I'm the one asking the questions here. I tried to think of some clever spiritual excuse for sitting on the steps instead of on the pews, but I couldn't find a holy fib, so I just told her the truth. "Sometimes I can take only so much of the church thing." I knew this truth would give her a free pass to heave stones at God and His church. I held my breath, waiting for her to go off on all that the church is not.

But her next words had nothing to do with the church. After I told the truth about playing hooky on the Holy, she said, "He hits me."

I quickly realized I had been pulled in way beyond the "Keep Out" sign. "Who hits you?" I asked.

"My husband," she slowly confessed. "He keeps hitting me, and hitting me in the head, and then a couple days ago he threw me down a flight of steps. I thought it was over. I thought I was going to die lying on the basement floor."

It was crazy. I'd just stuffed my soul with four days' worth of sermons, but none of them seemed to satisfy either of us right then. I apologetically whispered, "I'm so sorry."

She said, "No problem. I probably did something to deserve it. He says I always do. I walk by this place every day and have always wondered what it would be like to go in. Sometimes I wish churches didn't have stained glass windows so we could see what goes on in there every Sunday. I see all those folks dressed up so nice, and me ... well, I'm wearing my closet on my back. Don't think they would take too kindly to that."

The very church that had been the problem minutes earlier seemed like the only solution at that point. I thought there were several hours and plenty of pastors to fill them, so I invited her to come into the church as my guest.

She said with her head slumped over, "Sorry, I don't think so good. My thoughts get all jumbled up. I feel like I've been hit so many times I'm losing my mind. Anyways, those folks don't want me to dirty up their pretty little church."

I didn't preach a sermon but simply invited her in to hear one. I was praying she was wrong but feeling she might have been right. But she politely declined my invitation to come into the church that was all white, inside and out. I felt it had more to do with class than color, but either way she was right. We would have walked in, and some Bible bouncer would have posted the "Keep Out" sign in her face, justifying it with, "You probably wouldn't be comfortable here, but there is a church down the street you would feel more at ease in."

But that never happened because she didn't think the risk of rejection was worth the reward of restoration. I didn't blame her. I had witnessed way too many mumblings of church folks who take cheap shots at the poor and broken for their entertainment. "Did you see what she was wearing today? ... Yeah, I know ... I thought we were supposed to give God our best ... Well, if that's her best, I would hate to see her worst." I would have felt terrible to take her in just to have them tear her down. So I opted for church on the steps.

I asked if I could pray with her, and once again she answered me with silence. I said to myself, God, please help me help her.

After she had her fill of silence, she asked me the question that many ponder outside the stained glass. With all the courage she could muster, she asked, "Do you think God would ever listen to and love someone like me? I mean, would God ever hear my prayers, you know, someone who has been hit a lot?"

7

I tried to put her heart at ease, declaring, "Yes, yes, of course God loves you. He is madly in love with you."

"Really? Even if I have a not-so-good past?"

I loudly confirmed, "Especially people who have a not-so-good past." I quickly revealed what I normally conceal. "I too had a not-so-good past."

"But you're a pastor."

"Well, I was not born one, I became one."

She seemed to be stunned that a pastor could possibly have something in common with her.

Without bowing our heads or closing our eyes, I prayed a short prayer that God would help mend her mind and her marriage. When we stood up, there was something different about her. She looked me in the eye and smiled and thanked me for telling her that Jesus loved her. She perked up, saying, "I'm glad I came to church today."

"So am I, Patty."

How awesome was that? She thought she went to church, and her feet never smudged the marble floors. She never sat in a padded pew, and she didn't hear even one note from the pipe organ.

I chuckled as she walked down the sidewalk and passed the church's sign that bragged "Everybody is Welcome." I think Patty thought what many assume, that you were welcome if you looked like people in the church, made money like them, were the same color as them, and smelled the same as them.

I strolled back into my still vacant pew but not as impressed with the beauty of the building. How could the awe and wonder of a building be lost because of one conversation? I stared at the stained glass and wondered if anyone wondered what was on the other side of the glass. At times I would like to throw my hymnal through the stained glass ... not to let the light in but to let our light out.

As I gazed around the statuary, I witnessed hundreds of pastors taking meticulous notes on supersized sermons. I heard the secluded amens robotically recited on cue to the preacher's pitch and points. I saw smiling clergy selling libraries of their products in the back of the church, "Buy Two, Get One FREE." I saw manicured greeters with matching shirts and name tags. I still saw golden chandeliers, marble floors, padded pews, and that oversized pipe organ, but what I didn't see was Patty or anyone like her.

Don't misunderstand me; there's nothing evil about nice churches, Angel Soft toilet paper and sanctuaries crammed with fancy things unless they're used as bait to bring some in and keep others out. I believe saying one "Jesus Loves You" face-to-face to a stranger is worth far more than five days of sermons inside a church simply talking about it. I'm not sure what heaven looks like, but I think it looks a little more like cement steps than stained glass.

3
Everyone Has a Pen

What do Billy Graham, Charles Manson, Lady Gaga, the pope (any number), Elvis, Kirk Franklin, the Beatles, and you have in common? They all have pens. They write not with Bics or ballpoints but with the words, actions, deeds; they and we all daily journal in other people's lives.

In reality, everyone has a pen and everyone is an author. We all write into others peoples' stories by the things we do or don't do, so we are not only writing our own stories but are coauthoring our neighbors' narratives as well. Consciously or unconsciously we all make a difference each day by things done or undone, good or bad.

In a good way you may help a single mom pay her rent. You may visit a cancer patient in the hospital. You may go to your child's soccer game. You may tell your spouse you love them with a mammoth mound of chocolate or tickets to WrestleMania. Each person goes to bed at night remembering the things others did that made their life better. We all have pens; no one can stop us from scribbling a few gracious lines into someone else's story.

The pen may be used by an abusive father constantly cursing at his small child. It may be a seventy-year-old man exploiting a minor in a brothel. It may be someone walking into a liquor store and shooting the attrendeant because they wanted a free Snickers Bar. It may be reading a suicide note from your teenage daughter, who blames you for the funeral you are now planing. Everynight people go to bed knowing someone has broken into their stories, and they are forced to live with unwanted ink left on their pages.

Everyone, every day, has the power of the pen; every day as a parent and husband I journal into my wife's and two daughters' lives. When I'm in a good mood I have the pen. When I'm in a bad mood I have the pen. When I'm healthy I have the pen. When I'm sick I have the pen. When I feel like being a Christian I have the pen. When I don't feel like being a Christian I have the pen. Nobody gets a day without the pen.

Remember when Jesus' disciples came to Him and said, "Your friend Lazarus is dead"? Sorry to break the news to you, but Lazarus, his story was over; there was no hope. He had been dead for four days. People were morning and weeping as they were putting their pens back in their pockets. Jesus ignored the premature obituary, pulled out His pen, and began to write another chapter in Lazarus's life, starting with two words, "Come out." Jesus wrote not only into the stories in His day but also into all our stories, which have been changed and challenged by His story to help us write into others'.

For too long parishioners have surrendered their pens to priests, pastors, and prophets at the cost of libraries of blank pages in the folks around them. Too often church people think, "Let the pastor do it; his pen writes better than mine."

You have a pen, and even if you think you gave it away, you didn't. Even if you think someone stole it, no one did. Your pen continues to write even though it may be neatly tucked in your shirt pocket.

Here is just one example of someone who unexpectedly busted into my story. Several years ago God asked me to become a pastor; at the time I was making good money at a factory and doing just fine. I had a nice house on the water, a fast, red sports car, and money in the bank. After months of wrestling with God I finally gave in, quit my job, and went back to school.

How I am I going to pay for all the books and classes without a job? How will I pay for my dozen-a-day donut habit?

I sublimely thought God might recant His religious request. Oh, Dennis, I forgot about the money thing. Well, you better stay at the factory and save up a bit.

Nope, that didn't happen.

Okay, I'll go sign up next week, but they're going to think I'm a bit strange signing up for classes with no money.

That following Friday I received an unsigned letter in the mail crammed with cash. A typed note read, "Who I am is not important at this point. I heard you were going to school, and I am going to help you. You did something that changed my life, and this is my small way of saying thank you. God bless."

What? No name, no return address? Is there more where this came from? I wondered. What did I ever do to change someone's life? And how did they find out about my call into ministry when I'd just found out myself?

To this day I have no clue as to who took a pen and made a huge deposit in my account. Each week, as long as I was going to school, an envelope stuffed with cash folded in a blank piece of lined paper found its way into my mailbox.

That murky chapter in my life was made much clearer just because some anonymous person had written a few lines into my story each Friday. I don't know who that person is, but I want you and the world to hear how that person's story changed mine.

When God wants to change a life, seldom does He just show up with a magic wand, wave it, and chant, "Hocus-pocus, you're all better now." But He does show up every now and then by giving a pen to all kinds of people to squiggle a few words of grace and truth into the narrative of other peoples' lives.

Some of us feel we have to have a title or a position of influence to make a difference. Wrong! All we need to know is every day and everywhere we go we have a pen. We have the choice of what we write but not if we write. We can choose to use our pens to engrave good or evil, hope or hurt. But make no mistake about it—we are all authors, and we all have pens.

It's kind of funny how many times I have said, "I should write a book someday." But what I now realize is … I have. I have written a couple lines of hope at the soup kitchen. I have written libraries of good advice in my children's lives. (Well, I happen to think it was good advice.) I have written twenty years of love notes to my wife. I have written hundreds of sermons to bring light into the dark. I have written thousands of prayers to help mend people all around the world.

I have also written gossip that can never be erased. I have written jealousy to those I've envied. I have written hurt to those begging for help. I have written unforgiveness until they admit they are wrong. I have written lies to myself to justify my poor choices.

Every day we all splatter ink in all we do and say. You may not have a voice like Elvis, dance like Kirk Franklin, preach like Billy, or look good in a robe, but you have a pen—your pen. Tomorrow is a blank piece of paper just waiting for you to make your mark, so when you wake up each morning, know you have the power of the pen, not in your hand but in everything you do or don't do. Keep writing.

4
Those People

I was pinch-hitting for a friend, teaching a Wednesday night Bible study. It was a pretty tame group. I didn't think any of the folks had very high expectations of God or me. I found myself thinking sometimes we Christians attend midweek services more out of obligation than anticipation. I was sputtering along, teaching on a few elementary techniques on prayer.

After almost an hour you could tell my crew was planning an escape by their constant peeking at watches and the door. I didn't feel like it was one of my best performances and was ready to leave myself. It was a few minutes before our scheduled time of departure when people started to wake up, wipe the drool from their mouths, and shut their Bibles, universal signs that God and I had five minutes to wrap it up. I was sure some were thinking their nights could have been spent better watching "Wheel of Fortune" or "Jeopardy," and they probably would have learned more.

With only a few sentences left before I put a period on the evening, someone raised a hand. Because it was an adult class, it was a bit odd to see someone raise a hand like in elementary school. I thought maybe she had to go to the bathroom or something, so I smiled and nodded in her direction. She asked a question that bumped our Bible study into extra innings.

"How do you forgive a person you don't like?" she politely asked.

"Yeah, what if you hate someone? What if the person who hurt you won't admit it?" another added.

Before I could respond, others pitched in their two cents. "How do you forgive a person who abused you?" Five minutes earlier I had bored this class into a coma. Five minutes earlier they were wagging their tails in anticipation of being set free. Wait a minute! We're not talking about forgiveness! I tried shutting it down by telling them, "Great questions! You can explore it in depth next Wednesday when your real teacher is back."

I gave them all permission to scram, but they vetoed my early-release option. The class had perked up and was paying more attention to me than their watches. I began to travel down the dangerous dirt road of forgiveness. If you have ever taught a class on forgiveness, you know every question had a name and a story tethered to it. The once-docile class was starting to show fangs and getting a bit cranky about all the hurt they had collectively accumulated over the years. The previous fifty-five minutes I hadn't been able to get them to talk even if I had paid them, but right then they were firing questions faster than I could dodge them. They really wanted to know what we all want to know: How can we forgive those people who have damaged us without our permission?

I was in big, big trouble because some had just turned this Bible study into a courtroom, wanting revenge rather than restoration. Some were asking, "Is it right to pay them back for their sins against me?" I tried to play it by the book, calmly directing the mob back to Jesus' words in red, "Let's see what He says about forgiveness." Most wanted nothing to do with the red. They wanted revenge. The class was giving me a front-row seat to the emotional devastation that unforgiveness can cause.

I looked over to my left, and there was a guy the size of a Hummer wearing jeans and a patriotic red, white, and blue T-shirt. He was leaning against the wall in a metal chair, testing the back legs' weight limit. His eyes were closed, and his hands were drooping. I chalked it up to my ability to put another saint to sleep simply by teaching. The other members of the class were still playing judge and jury, prosecuting absent villains for past felonies. I did my best to give the group what the Bible and I had on forgiveness. It was not adequate for most of the folks, but a few retracted their fangs and calmed down.

They all got up and left the room, except one snoring giant still weighing down his grey metal chair. I let him rest as I was erasing the board. He flopped his chair down on all fours, ready to fight someone. Without raising his hand he raised his voice. "No, I'm not going to do it." This puzzled me because the class was over and I had never said anything to him. He repeated with even more fury in his voice, "There is no way I will forgive those people!"

It looked like the Jolly Green Giant hadn't been sleeping after all. Up to that point people had had enough grace not to mention any one of those people by name, but I had a real strange feeling that was about to change. I wanted to go home. I knew this was bigger than what I had written on the board that night. After all, I was just a sub, not the main guy. I tiptoed into his world, asking, "Who are those people?"

His mind instantly traveled back to the sixties, and flashbacks were popping up faster than he could erase them. He began to sweat, narrating what it had been like serving in Vietnam. He was now the teacher; I was the student. I let him and his flashbacks take the lead.

He talked about walking into villages and watching his friends being ambushed. He said, "I have seen too much, way too much to just forget and forgive. When you were talking about forgiveness, I closed my eyes and saw their faces. It's been decades, and I still see the faces of the scumbags that killed my buddies. Tonight, when you talked about forgiveness, it was like I was there all over again. I could hear the bullets and bombs, see the puddles of blood in the rice fields. I would go back to my tent at night with my boots plastered in mud and blood of both their boys and ours. It was the first time I ever saw a dead body outside of a casket. I could hear the desperate cries of twenty-year-old boys crying out for their moms and Jesus in that order. I seldom sleep without being forced awake by the sights and sounds of the sixties. I'm still carrying around lead in my hips as a parting gift from 'Nam and those people."

"I thought when I reached stateside all those memories would stay in the fields, but they didn't; they follow me wherever I go. So forgive me for not forgiving them, but there's no chance I'll forgive those people for the damage they caused my buddies and me. You can preach all you want about what the red verses in the Bible say, but I can't do it. You stand up there telling us we need to forgive everybody for everything. I disagree. I feel there are some people so bad in this world they don't deserve to be forgiven. I have too many scars, drank too many shots, and had too many sleepless nights to let those people off the hook."

I wanted to ask, Do you not see what not forgiving those people is doing to your mind? Don't you see you are the POW? I wanted to stand on a soapbox and preach a healing sermon on forgiveness. But he would have said, "You weren't there, and you have no clue what I experienced!"

And he would have been right. While he was fighting for our country, I was fighting for five extra yards on a high school football field. While he was watching men die, I was watching cartoons. He was so angry; it had been over forty years that his body had been free, and forty years that his mind hadn't. He was, like some other vets I have met, handcuffed to his past without the key.

When Jesus asked us to forgive, He sure had a few of those people in his own life: those people who lie more than love; those people who criticize more than cheer; those people who hate more than help; those people who ditch ya' when it gets tough, those people who crucified an innocent man. The guards were plunging thorns into his head, nails into his hands, and a spear into his side. They had beaten Him so badly that He was unrecognizable to His friends (what few He had left). People were punching, laughing, and mocking Him just for fun. Jesus knew about those people who made it almost impossible to forgive.

But Jesus said something that caught the fuming mob by surprise. In his dying moments He gave them a gift they hadn't asked for, forgiveness. He gave them a gift they thought they never needed. Before He died He wanted the good religious people who had pummeled Him to know they were forgiven.

This had to leave the guards scratching their helmets, thinking, We ripped the flesh off his bones and beat him till we were out of breath. Why would this guy do that? I think He did it to show the whole world we would always have those people in our lives.

Nobody goes through life without wearing the unwanted scars of those people. Jesus knew when we don't forgive others it's we who pay the highest price—peace of mind. We have a tendency if we choose to forgive to do so after some time has passed and the wounds have begun to heal. But Jesus forgave those people while they were still killing Him. This clearly confused a few of the spectators that day, and even a few of the workers.

Can you imagine one of the guards going home after work that day? His five-year-old daughter meets him at the door, runs up, and jumps into his arms. She asks him what she always asks him, "Daddy, daddy, how was your day at work? What did you do?" Then she asks him a question he will never forget, "Daddy, what's that red stuff all over your hands?"

He stumbles for an answer a five-year-old can understand. He looks down and sees Jesus' blood now smudged on his daughter's white dress. He begins to cry.

"Daddy? What's wrong? Why are you crying? Did I do something wrong?"

He replies, "No, honey. Daddy did something wrong, really wrong." Then he remembers those last words Jesus whispered out loud, loud enough for the whole world to hear, "Forgive them." Hours ago they meant nothing. Hours ago he laughed when He offered him, offered us, forgiveness. He'd thought, "This guy has lost his mind. Who forgives someone who's trying to kill you?"

Though that guard and a Vietnam vet were separated by over two thousand years, they both were standing at the same spot. They were standing at that place where they had a choice. It was a place packed with those people. Those people who have hurt us ... Those people who have lied to and about us ... Those people who have sucker punched us for just trying to help ... Those people who have abandoned us at our weakest moments … Those people who are the ones Jesus died for … Those people who we have the choice to forgive or spend the rest of our lives chained to.

A choice—that's where I was on that Wednesday night, offering a vet the key to uncuff himself from his past. Anyone who says forgiveness is easy has never worn the scars of those people. Forgiveness is never easy, but it is right. I was offering him what Jesus offered those people and us people, an opportunity to forgive and be forgiven. You could tell he was not ready to give up on his forty-year-old flashbacks, at least not that night. He stood up and walked out of the church as broken as he had walked in.

I wanted to run and tackle him in the parking lot, to pin him to the pavement until he forgave those people. I wanted to put him in a full nelson until he cried "Uncle!" and forgave those people. The problem was twofold; he was 153 pounds heavier, and over the years I've learned you can't force forgiveness on anyone. That night many in the class went home and watched "Jeopardy" while he limped home and watched forty-year-old reruns of 'Nam in his head.

I saw him dozens of times after that night, but he always talked about sports, politics, and the price of gas. He pretended the whole forgiveness thing had never happened. I wish I could neatly tie this story up with an amazing testimony about how he forgave those people. That didn't happen as far as I know. Each day he probably still wakes up and presses "play" to watch forty-year-old reruns, always ending the same way: "I hate those people."

Jesus had those people, my friend had those people, and you and I have those people. People who make forgiveness look as attractive as Brussels sprouts to a four-year-old. It's funny, but some of the very people I label as those people are the same people who label me as one of those people.

I will resist the strong urge to get all preachy on you. The fact is we all have blown it in some areas of our lives. I too have those people in my life who make forgiveness much easier to preach than to practice. At times I brag to God that I have forgiven someone until I see them in aisle ten at Walmart. Then my inner linebacker bursts out in me, wanting to tackle that particular person and put them in a full nelson until they ask me for forgiveness.

I know, I know—you can't force forgiveness but we can offer and receive it.

5

Scoreboards

It was one of the worst days of my life. I was standing in front of my mom's casket after cancer had chalked up another win on its dreadful résumé. I didn't know how to act or respond. I had never had someone I love so much die. I'd known this punch was coming, but I hadn't known how much it would hurt. I felt like that day caused a scar even time will struggle to heal.

You know what I mean if you have lost people who have left more than just wills behind. They left libraries stocked full of memories that will never be forgotten. Funerals are a tricky road to navigate. Most of us have watched hundreds of people drive that dark stretch of pavement, but until you're behind the wheel you really don't understand.

Having been a pastor for many years now, I've done hundreds of funerals witnessed by thousands of people. Sometimes people have such dysfunctional relationships that their funerals are more like wrestling matches than memorial services. I've done funerals during which fights have broken out in the parking lot over who would get a bigger chunk of the inheritance, and I've had people come up and ask me to referee their family feuds.

Once I did a funeral for a World War II vet in a small town. I was at the cemetery with the funeral director, waiting for the family to show up. I waited and waited, thinking maybe traffic had been backed up or maybe a flat tire had caused the uncomfortable delay.

After several more minutes passed, I asked the director, "Who's coming?"

He said, "Sorry, I forgot to tell you. Nobody called when he died. There will be no one showing up. No one claimed the body."

So feeling he deserved a service nonetheless, I stood over his headstone and did the service with no one there.

I've performed funerals in which the deceased had left huge voids in the world. They were people who had lived their lives with their legacies in mind. They had spent most of their lives serving God and loving others. The funeral homes wouldn't have enough chairs to seat all who they'd left behind.

That was my mom's funeral. She'd left no money to quibble over, only memories to cherish. As I stood on guard I couldn't believe how many memories were flooding my mind. Things from when I was a kid that had meant nothing to me at the time became priceless; life lessons I'd thought I'd ignored or forgotten were demanding my attention.

Before all those hundreds of funerals, there was a first. I'd never thought when I was going into ministry that my mom would be that funeral—the first. I was a rookie pastor, which only confused my emotions more as to how I should respond. On the one hand I didn't want to give God a black eye for what He had allowed, but His DNA was all over this mess; if He had the power to heal cancer and had not, that seemed to be on Him. I was disappointed with God for pulling her out of the game so early; she'd been only fifty-three. Though that seemed ancient then, I'm that same age now, and I know it's really young. I didn't get it. I'd prayed, fasted, gone to church three times a week, given a dime on the dollar. I'd lived the best life I could, and still He had said no to me and my prayers. Because I was a new pastor I thought maybe I had done something wrong.

I wrestled the night before the funeral with what version of Dennis Cook to show off to the public the next day: my mom's son or the world's pastor. Something must have clogged up my mind that night because I ended up picking the wrong one. The next day I suited up in my pastor's costume and grabbed my Bible and two sprays of cologne, and I was off to one of the worst days of my life.

I showed up and greeted everyone with some well-rehearsed verse about God and His perfect will. I kept half a smile glued to my face to let people know God was still in control. Hundreds of people asked me, "How are you doing?"

I served up three fibs to everyone gullible enough to swallow them: "God's in control … God has a plan … She's in a better place." All these lies were true but not true for me, at least not that day. I didn't like the lying thing, but it beat having a meltdown in front of my family and friends.

People were so impressed with my trio of lies and my pretending to be spiritually mature. Some were patting me on the back, telling me what a great

Christian example I was to them and God. Others praised my poise, especially being such a new pastor. Every time I wanted to cry I forced myself to stay in character and be strong for my family and friends. I mentally kept repeating to myself, Real pastors don't cry. I wanted the world to know God was real and could help us in the worst days of our lives. The problem was the longer I played out this lie the sicker I became.

Thoughts kept running through my head. I know I should be more spiritual and just accept this knockout punch like a good little Christian solider, but I'm hurt. God, I want my mom back now! You raised Lazarus from the dead, so why can't you raise my mom?

Something in me wanted to grab the microphone so heaven could hear me screaming in the middle of the funeral I'm so mad at God right now! I don't think He is in control. I don't think He has a plan at all! Yes, my mom may have been in a better place, but I felt trapped in the worst.

I wanted to throw all the beautiful flowers through the window. I wanted to flip over all the coffee tables full of four-by-six pieces of paper with my mom's whole life crammed onto them. I wanted to lie on floor and cry like a baby who had just lost his bottle. I didn't want to read the Twenty-third Psalm. I wanted to swear. The truth kept screaming to be set free, but fear caused me to duct tape its mouth to protect the lie and my Christian image.

I felt as though I had lost one of the only cheerleaders I'd ever had who hadn't cared if I won or lost in life. She was gone. My mom never paid much attention to the scoreboards. Back in high school our basketball team was, well, let's just say not state champs. There were games we'd be down 247 to 5 with two minutes left, and I can still hear my mom's voice filling up the gym, "C'mon, Dennis! We can do it! Don't give up, honey!"

Honey may have worked on the ball diamond when I was five but not in the high school gym. I remember thinking, I'm a man now! Don't call me honey! I remember the guys on the bench (where I spent most of my time) saying, "Cookie, your mom is crazy. Can't she read the scoreboard? We're getting slaughtered!"

Being an eleventh-grade benchwarmer trying to protect my reputation, I'd go along with them. "Yeah, my mom's not too good with math." Back then I was so embarrassed that she kept screaming that her boy was number one when my Chuck Taylors barely ever touched the dusty gym floor.

She would try to stir up the fizzling fans, trying to get them to do some obnoxious cheer she had stolen from the fifties. Her cheering got so loud and out of control during one game that the boys were teasing me without remorse.

I cornered her after the game and scolded her. "Mom, you got to stop with all those number-one chants when we're losing a million to one!"

She smiled and said, "Oh, I'm sorry if I embarrass you, but how are you going to make a comeback if no one cheers you on?"

"Mom, you just have to stop."

"Okay, honey, I'll tone it down a bit."

Well, the next game, and the next game, and the next game, and all the games after that she never toned it down. She felt it was her God-given mission to be my personal cheerleader.

Well, after a lifetime of being my public cheerleader, she had finally said yes to my high school scolding and had stopped cheering. We have no idea of the power of personal cheerleaders until their voices have been silently tucked into caskets. I would walk on hot coals all the way back to that old high school gym for just one more game just to be able to hear her deafening voice. That time, when my mom would go into her "We're number one" rants, when she would start screaming for us to not give up, I would stand up and cheer with her.

And when my bench buddies would start teasing me, "Cookie, you and your mom are both crazy! We're losing a million to one!" I would say, "Oh, I'm sorry if we're embarrassing you, but how are we going to make a comeback if no one cheers us on?"

Not only did she cheer on her own kids but other peoples' kids as well. If they were losing, my mom was cheering. Every Christmas my mom would invite people over who may have not had life's scoreboards tilted in their favor. I remember asking her, "Mom, why do always invite all these people over on Christmas when it's a family day?" She would respond, "Because everybody doesn't have family."

The day of her funeral I felt like I was losing a million to one. I kept looking up in the bleachers and down at her casket and I couldn't see or hear her voice, and it was killing me. I, like so many kids, had taken her voice for granted. I just thought she would always be in the stands. I thought her and her cheers would never stop. But I was wrong.

It seemed stupid standing in front of a dead woman's casket wishing for her to talk. I wanted her to tell me I was going to make it through this mess. I wanted to her tell me I was going to be a good dad and husband. I wanted her to tell me one more time that I was not a screwup no matter what my scoreboard said. I wanted her to tell me she loved me one more time because in spite of the million times she'd told me that before, I always thought I'd get one more.

I stood at the front of that casket for hours, but it felt like years. Everyone kept asking me how I was doing, and I just kept on lying. It was funny how all those people surrounded me, telling me they loved me, but I felt all alone because the person I wanted to hear it from the most couldn't talk.

Mom, I know I can't hear your voice, but if you can hear mine, there are a few things I want to say to you. First, I'm sorry I was so embarrassed by your public displays of love. I was more concerned with my reputation than your feelings. I would give anything to hear your very loud voice telling me not give up. Mom, there have been so many times over the years when I almost ended it because when I looked up at my scoreboard it had just announced to the world what a loser I was. You always told me you loved me even when I didn't love myself. Looking back now, it seems as though there was nothing I could do bad enough to get you to stop cheering.

You would love the little church we started. It's called the Restoration Station. It's a cool place where broken people can come as they are no matter what their scoreboards say. Each week I try to cheer them on, telling them not to give up even if they're down a million to one. Sound familiar?

About being a dad, I love it! Cancer stole your chance of ever meeting your granddaughters, Mackenzie and Morgan, but you would be so proud of them. They are both champions for the underdogs in life.

I kept telling them at their sporting events, "You think I embarrass you? You better be glad Grandma Cook isn't here, because if she were, all you teammates would be saying, 'Who's that crazy old lady up in the stands?'"

You would get a kick out of the fact that I regularly embarrass my two girls by chasing them down in front of all their friends, telling them how much I love them. Yes, they cringe and run the other way, totally embarrassed. But who cares, right? Each Christmas our family drags out extra seats because someone told me everybody doesn't have family.

Mom, I have traveled all around the world and have seen some horrible injustices; so many people are hauling around scoreboards with no hope of ever making any comebacks. They have no "crazy people" like you in their bleachers making a fool of themselves by chanting "Don't give up! You're number one!" I want you to know I've not gotten to them all, but I've gotten to a few. I've made a fool of myself recycling your old cheer, "Don't give up; you're number one no matter what your scoreboard says!"

I miss you almost as much as I love you. By now I'm sure God has already given you tons of trophies for being such a great mom to us kids. I do know you're in a better place, and I will be too if I can just remember your voice. Out of libraries of lessons you left for me I remember two of them the most. One, we all deserve a crazy person in the bleachers cheering us on no matter what the scoreboard says. And two, it's okay to be bad at math.

Miss ya … Den

The story you just read I shared with our church on Mother's Day on May 13, 2012, as a tribute to her and all those like her. When I concluded the reading of the story I thought it was going to be therapeutic and help ease the pain of missing her. Instead it was the opposite; I ended up craving her and her cheers even more. People walked out crying and giving their thanks and saying it reminded them of their moms. As for me, it left me wanting more than a tribute. I wanted her.

Before church started that day, a woman handed me a small gift. She said, "Sorry, I've been storing this for a while, but I always keep forgetting to bring it to you."

I thanked her and tossed it onto the pulpit and forgot about it.

After the service everyone was gone except my wife and me. I told her that I'd better grab that gift before I left. It was tucked inside a plastic sandwich bag wrapped in a white paper napkin. When I opened it I saw a painted clay angel about four inches tall, nice as angels go. As a pastor I received a lot of nice little gifts from the folks at our church. I decided I would hang it in my office somewhere. But something made me turn it over, and that's when I almost passed out. I looked down, and etched into the clay on the back was my mom's name. She had been dead for over twenty years at that time. I almost lost my legs with sheer shock and gratitude; it took my breath away. I felt I was holding my mother's spirit in the palm of my hands. I think I said a thousand times, "How can this be?" After showing my wife and daughters, they lost it too, crying tears of awe and joy with me. I will always label that day as the Mother's Day Miracle Sunday.

It was such a gift to hear my mom's "voice" after twenty years of silence. Somehow, this trinket my mom had made when she was a girl had survived decades of being shuffled around from one stranger to the next, but that day it found its final resting place. I have all kinds of expensive junk flung all over our house, but the clay angel, which probably cost all of seventy-five cents to make, has taken cuts on all my possessions and is now one of my most valuable. I hung that priceless angel, named Joan Cook, above our fake fireplace as a reminder that people may die but their voices live. It is one of the greatest Mother's Day gifts I have ever gotten. To be honest, it's the only Mother's Day gift I have ever gotten.

Who knows? Maybe my mom heard me after all and is still the crazy old lady in heaven's bleachers, still cheering me on.

6

Crazy Man

I love to venture out on prayer walks throughout our community; I never know what will happen. Prayer walking is simply walking and praying about anything you see or feel.

One day a friend and I hit the streets to pray for anything and everything. We picked a street that had several folks sifting the nooks and crannies for empty cans and handouts. It was a great day of praying for businesses, restaurants, schools, and people who were out and about. On our way back to the church, we were walking through a parking lot when we saw a very animated man walking toward us. He was the type who's probably defined more by description than name. He was the guy you warned your kids to walk around. One pant leg was rolled up while the other dragged the ground. His long, coarse hair was flopping out of a multicolored stocking cap. A star-spangled do-rag was wrapped around his neck. He sported a pair of supersized, black sunglasses that covered most of his sunburned face. He was pushing a scooter, mumbling loud enough to be heard but not clear enough to be understood. My bet was that nobody could get through to him, and there was probably nobody losing much sleep over him.

As he approached, we politely said, "Hi!"

He loudly interrupted our introduction with a rant of random questions. "Where were you when the space shuttle went down, man? Can you fix your own transmission? Do you know how much a gallon of milk costs? Do you know what high school I went to?"

Before we could give a guesstimate, he blasted off to another planet of dead presidents, global warming, interest rates, and a galaxy of other miscellaneous facts.

I love to go on prayer walks, meet complete strangers going through difficult times, and spontaneously pray with them. Many times the people will be overwhelmed with emotion at the conclusion of the prayer, saying things like, "Wow, I can't believe you would pray with someone like me, and we aren't even in church!"

That time I almost took a rain check on praying with the confussed man. What's the use? He has no ability to comprehend anything we've said let alone a prayer. This man has clearly lost his mind. We've been talking for minutes without hearing one syllable of logic that would suggest he knew we're here. I know God loves everybody, but what good is love if you can't understand it? Well, what do I have to lose?

I looked him in the eyes and asked, "Sir, can I pray with you?"

He rigidly clasped his hands at his waist and straightened up like he was in the military. I launched out into a prerecorded prayer about hope and help. I was praying more out of a sense of duty than desire, but somewhere in the middle of my prayer something happened. I felt it. God's presence gently busted into my boring prayer. It was no longer my words but His. I felt God loved this man and wanted him to know it. I concluded my brief prayer by reassuring him that God loved him.

When I finished praying, I looked up. I'll never forget what I saw. He was standing at attention, tears dripping down his cheeks. He slowly removed his gigantic glasses and calmly said, "Thank you. I understood every word you said." He hung his glasses back on his head and reached into his pocket, sifting for something.

We asked, "Do you need some money?"

Ignoring our question, he pulled out a couple of crinkled-up bills and change; he caught us both off-guard by asking, "Do I need to pay you for that prayer?"

"What do you mean?"

"That nice prayer you prayed. Do I have to pay for it?"

I quickly put his mind at ease. "No. That one's on the house."

Instantly he slipped back into whatever world he called home. He picked right up where he had left off, flinging pointless data into the air as he and his scooter zipped around us.

The prayer did not save him. The prayer did not make him rich. The prayer did not give him his mind back. To be truthful, I'm not sure what that prayer did for him, but I do know what it did for me. It taught me. Just because a crazy man doesn't understand me doesn't mean he doesn't understand God. Our prayers are not just us talking to people but us talking to God for people. Prayer is always more powerful than the person who prays it.

7
Waiting to Be Seated

I walked into a Coney Island restaurant only to be greeted by a sign that read, "Please wait to be seated." You find this type of sign in almost any restaurant that doesn't dole out plastic silverware. They are posted to make sure us patrons don't just walk in and pick any ol' seat we want. Most of the time I obey the sign unless my belly is on E, then I slip past it, pretending it doesn't apply to me.

I waited till the coast was clear and casually detoured around the sign. That time my little trick didn't work. A waitress who had borrowed Hulk Hogan's biceps told me to get back in line and wait my turn. I wanted to protest, but it would not have looked good in the local newspaper to read, "Pastor Gets a Beat-Down by Angry Waitress," so I agreed.

I was sure this trying to sneak past the Hulk and the sign had violated some hidden rule buried in the Bible, so I asked God to forgive me and to speed up the line. Just when I finally made amends with God this snappily dressed fella came strutting in with a paper tucked under his arm, greeting the waitress by her first name.

She flirtingly said, "Good morning, Bill. You want your usual seat?" He walked around me and the sign straight to his table stocked with his hot coffee just the way he liked it—two creams and a sugar.

Hey, buddy! Can't you read the sign? I tried that and almost got tossed out!

After waiting for hours (okay, three minutes, but it seemed like hours), I was escorted to a coffeeless seat. A few minutes later a pastor friend of mine joined me for a couple of Coneys and some church chat. We began to talk about God, church, and a mission trip my daughter and I were going on.

I looked over my friend's shoulder and noticed a middle-aged man wearing a black hoodie under a faded blue-jean jacket eavesdropping on our conversation. When I'd look at him he would turn his head away, but each time I looked his way he was looking ours. I thought maybe the volume or of our conversation or content was bothering him. We kept volleying our opinions back and forth on how to make the church more effective in our communities. After an hour or so of solving all the world's problems, we were ready to give up our seats to the next person the Hulk and her twenty-four-inch guns had detained behind the sign.

As we were getting ready to slide out of our seats, we looked up, and the eavesdropper was standing like a barricade at the end of our table. He introduced himself. "Hello, my name is Kevin. Are you churchgoing people?"

We both tried to camouflage our pastoral credentials by simply saying, "You could say that." We were not embarrassed to admit we were pastors, but when you tell some people you're a pastor, they sometimes become instantly religious or start confessing sins, theirs and others.

And that's what happened. He began to tell us about his nasty divorce as if he were on the Jerry Springer show. He gushed out his brokenness more like a fire hydrant than a faucet. He exposed piles of dirty details that would have made the National Enquirer blush. His volume cranked up from easy listening to heavy metal with every sentence. His tone and topic were drawing the ears and eyes of the whole restaurant (okay, maybe just a few noisy people around us).

He had no clue his voice was carrying, but even if he had, I don't think he would have cared anyway. He wanted the whole world to know he had been taken to the cleaners. I think he was a lonely, broken man having a midlife meltdown and just wanted to tell his side of the story. There were so many places my friend and I wanted to slap on Band-Aids of wisdom, but we just let him bleed for now.

After minutes of justified ranting, he lowered his voice a few octaves and then unapologetically began to rat out his ex-church. He told us that when he had divorced his wife, his church had divorced him. No one from the church actually walked up and said, "Hey, Kevin, we want a divorce, so leave." No, that would have taken too much honesty. What they did instead was stop talking to him and start talking about him. They stopped sitting with him and started sitting around him. After years of rejection from his wife and his church, he agreed to divorce them both.

God must have been gnawing at his conscience, because three years after his split with his church and his wife he woke up one Sunday with a plan to kiss and make up with the church. If that went well, who knows what could happen in his marriage? His logic was that he would run back to God before walking back to his wife. He was not sure if he was motivated by guilt or God, but either way he figured it was time.

So he sifted through his closet looking for his Sunday suit, blowing off three years of dust and shame from lack of use. He tiptoed into a new church full of old memories and hoped for a fresh start. He plastered on a Sunday smile and tried to blend in with all the happy people.

A peppy greeter at the door flung out his right hand with a well-rehearsed, "Good morning, glad you're here this morning."

He knew the routine, so he played along, shaking his hand, responding, "Thank you, so am I."

With one question the greeter morphed into a Sherlock Holmes. "What brings you in to our church today?"

There was no way he would tell him the truth, fearing being bounced out before he even got in. He faked a smile and pleaded the fifth. He walked into the service trying to sneak into a back pew; that way he could make a quick getaway in case God was still fuming at him for skipping church the last three years. He tapped a gentleman on his shoulder, expecting him to move over. His first tap ignored, he tapped a bit more deliberately.

The saint stoically twisted his head to the right, looked at him as if he were the Antichrist, and barked out four words like a lieutenant to a private: "This is my seat!"

At that point those four words ripped open a three-year-old scab. He wanted to turn around and run but had no place to run to; he decided he needed God more than he needed that seat. So he limped up a few more pews, trying one more time. He tapped on another man's shoulder, making sure he felt it.

Well, the good thing was he didn't ignore him; the bad thing was he told him, "I have been sitting in this seat for thirty years and I am not moving now."

He could not believe this! He understood a sign at a Coney Island restaurant forcing him to wait to be seated, but at a church? He informed my friend and me that he left and was never going back. That was years ago. He gave us a pop quiz.

"That's wrong, right? Is that the way you are supposed to be treated in church? You guys are pastors. What did I do wrong? I did what I felt God asked me to do. I can't imagine how they would have treated me if I'd chosen to be honest and told Holmes I was divorced!"

My friend and I did not deny or defend his story; we just listened. We both had heard this story play out multiple times in churches all around the world.

He said, "It just doesn't seem fair to get shunned by the people who brag about how much they love the lost. Crazy! I'm as lost as lost can get, and if I can't find a seat, who can?"

Still standing, he put his pain on pause and asked us right there in the Coney Island what he asked the saints in church. "Can I sit with you?"

My friend slid over, and he plopped down, exhaling the words, "Thanks you for letting me sit with you." We let him download decades of damage and frustration.

When he took a breath, I asked him, "Can we pray for you?"

He replied yes silently with the bowing of his head. I began to pray, but he interrupted me, asking us if we could please hold his hands while we prayed. It was a very short prayer reminding him God was not mad at him and encouraging him to give the church thing another try.

My buddy said, "I have a church a stone's throw from here if you would like to come. I promise I'll save you a seat."

He thought that was funny coming from a pastor. The prayer and invitation seemed to have stopped the bleeding, at least for the time being.

He exited our makeshift confessional booth telling us, "Well, ya never know, guys, but I may be there one Sunday."

I don't know if he showed up or not, but I do know he was willing to give God another chance to give him another chance.

I wondered, after he left, how many people every week walk into a church hungry for healing and hope only to be greeted by a hidden sign reading "Please Wait to be Seated" and some spiritual gorilla at the door telling them:

Please wait until you get your act together ...

Please wait until you and your spouse kiss and make up ...

Please wait until you quit your nasty habits ...

Please wait until you get caught up on your tithing ...

Please wait until you have nicer clothes ...

Please wait until you ask God for forgiveness ...

You might be thinking, "Dennis, I think your hyperbole has gotten the best of you. That stuff doesn't happen in church these days."

All you have to do is plunk your nose down in the book of James chapter 2 and read four sentences and you will see the same thing. Two thousand years ago James was ticked off because a Bill had strolled into church dressed in a suit and tie with the Wall Street Journal tucked under his arm and got ushered past the rest to box seats. When Kevin crawled in, they told him, "Sorry, dude, you'll have to sit on the floor. There's no room."

As long as there are the haves and the have nots, the haves will always hear, "Good morning, Bill! You want your usual seat?" And it will be fully stocked with hot coffee just the way they like it. The have nots will hear, "I've been sitting in this seat for thirty years and I am not moving now."

James and God are not frustrated with people who have money; several Bible folks had sizable checking accounts. It's the fact that they thought their money bought them season tickets to front-row seats while the rest of the poor people, oh well …

Every Sunday is the first Sunday in church for some people. No matter whose fault, their lives have tragically fallen apart; they don't know where the bathrooms are, they don't know anyone's first name, and they don't have anyone to sit with. All they know is the sign out front read, "Everybody Welcome."

So if you are asked to give up your seat to a visitor this Sunday, even if you have had your backside glued to it for thirty years, please slide over. Is your seat worth losing someone like Kevin? Every Sunday is someone's first Sunday, but my buddy and I learned every Sunday is also some folks' last Sunday, because sometimes people just get tired of waiting for a seat.

8

Detroit Tigers Jacket

I was eager to meet a friend I hadn't seen in a while for lunch. It was a cool, fall day, perfect temperature to sport my brand-new, official, Detroit Tigers blue-and-white jacket. I'm a lifelong Tigers fan and proud of it. It was the coat the Tigers had worn during the season; it cost a hundred and fifty dollars I didn't have, and it was worth every thread of it.

The lunch meeting was one of the first times I'd proudly unveiled my new jacket to the public. I strutted into the restaurant like I played for the team, my chest swollen, trying to fill my new XL coat. I know this sounds very shallow, but I loved that jacket.

After walking only a few steps into the restaurant, a waiter with the waist of a number-two pencil and the height of a telephone pole spotted me. He trotted over, swinging up his right hand, waiting for a high five. I slapped his bony fingers, playing along, thinking, Who is this overly friendly stranger? My famished ego thought, "Maybe he thinks I play for the Tigers with my new jacket on."

He asked, "Hey man, where did you get that coat?"

As you might guess, I was more than willing to drag him through a play-by-play of my coat purchase story. I told him where I had gotten it and how much it had cost, and I assured him it was no knockoff but the real deal.

He verbally applauded my new jacket, saying, "I love that jacket." He smiled and said, "I think that coat would look good on me." I immediately dismissed his joke with a counterfeit laugh and gave him directions to the sports store where he could get his own.

He replied, "I think I might do that after work today."

"I didn't catch your name."

"Mike."

"Okay, Mike, good talking with you, and good luck on your new jacket."

I slipped into the bathroom to wash my hands. I was still glowing from the praise he'd pitched my and my jacket's way. Then I heard what I thought was God talking to me about my coat. Wow, even heaven wants to toss a little praise my jacket's way. If you can't tell, I loved my new jacket.

My brief glow was snuffed out with one sentence from heaven. Dennis, I want you to give that waiter your jacket.

I balked. "No way, God! I love this jacket. I'm not giving him my new coat." Arguing out loud, I was glad I was the only one in the bathroom. While God and I were bartering over my new jacket, I told Him, I bought this coat fair and square with my own money, plus I have been saving up all year to buy it.

Yeah, I know, but I want him to have your coat.

I disagreed with the call, reminding God that guy would have to eat three dozen cheeseburgers to fill out my extra-large jacket. "God, I don't even know this guy, plus you heard him say he was going to buy his own jacket right after work."

I quickly put an end to the give-your-jacket-to-a-stranger chatter by storming out of the bathroom with my jacket zipped up to my nose. I sat with my friend, who had been patiently waiting through this divine pilfering of my prize possession. We talked about our ministries, families, and a few current events. Then almost on heaven's cue he asked, "Dennis, I really like your jacket. Is it new?"

That time, less than eager to dive into the details, I just mumbled, "Yep."

After a half an hour or so of chitchat, my friend interrupted, "Dennis, there's a guy over there staring and smiling at us."

I didn't have to turn my head to know it was the number-two pencil still trying to steal my new coat. I snuck a peek to my left to verify my hunch, and there he was, beaming from ear to ear, waving at me like a politician in a parade.

Doesn't this guy have some tables to wait on or something?

My friend questioned, "Dennis, what's going on?"

I fessed up to the whole hearing voices in the bathroom thing. I told him, "I think God wants me to give Slim my jacket, my new jacket."

"What are you going to do?"

"I have two choices. One, obey God and give him my coat, or two, ignore God and the number-two pencil and keep my jacket. I guess I'm going to pick one and give him my jacket, but I want the record to show I'm not happy about it."

After an hour or so of kicking and screaming with and at God, I gave up. I felt a bit guilty about my childish overreaction to my coat. But hey, it wasn't any old coat! It was the official coat of the Detroit Tigers.

I slowly slipped off my coat and emptied my pockets on the table. I knew it was the right call, but it certainly wasn't the easy one. I took a napkin on the table and wrote the waiter a brief note. I wrote, "I just want you to know that God has heard your prayers. God has great plans for your life. Don't give up on hope." I wrote the words more like a holy hunch than a prophetic truth.

I slid out of my booth, looking for the waiter to see if he even wanted my coat. I spotted him, and he came running across the restaurant and stood in front of me.

I said in a monotone voice, "I feel God has asked me to give you my jacket, but if you feel that would be inappropriate for an on duty waiter to confiscate a customer's coat and leave him freezing in the cold, I would completely understand."

Before I could finish giving him a way out, the light pole hollered down, "Of course I'll take it! I love that jacket."

I thought, What kind of law-abiding citizen would have the nerve to accept a complete stranger's jacket? He reached out to grab my, I mean his, new coat. I gripped the coat, almost making him tug it out of my hands. This is crazy. I have to pay ten bucks for lunch, plus a tip, and hand over a hundred-and-fifty-dollar coat. If I walk out of here coatless and I find out that voice was not God's, I'm going to be ticked at someone.

Before heading back out into the cold, coatless world, I remembered the napkin note. I handed him the folded thoughts on his future.

"What's this?" He read the note and his face morphed from joy to shock. He stood there with dazzled eyes, staring at me questioning, "How did you know? How did you know what I was praying for? There's no way you could have known that!"

I didn't immediately answer the question partly because I didn't know; it had been just a hunch. He confessed he had been privately praying at night that God would give him another shot at hope. He lamented that his poor choices had disqualified him from God's team and his dreams. At that point we both realized the moment was bigger than a hunch and a jacket.

I strongly argued that God still had a spot for him on His team. I asked, "If you don't mind, what was it that you have been praying about at night?"

With no hesitation he said, "I want to own my own restaurant."

I cheered, "Wow, that's awesome! What kind?"

"A fancy steak joint. There's none around this area." He went on and on, forgetting he was on still on the clock; it was so cool hearing a dream that had been cooped up in bedtime prayers for years. He said, "I'm so glad God sent you to me today." I smiled and told Mike I'd keep an eye out for his fancy steak place.

As I walked out of the restaurant I glanced back and saw one of the most beautiful pictures I had seen in a long time, Mr. Number-Two Pencil still standing and staring at a napkin soaked with a half-dozen inked words of hope like it was the Bible.

It was then I realized the whole adventure had nothing to do with a hundred-and-fifty-dollar, official Detroit Tigers jacket but everything to do with a free napkin. God loved this waiter so much that He had given him a napkin gift wrapped in a Detroit Tigers jacket.

When I got back in my truck I was once again reminded of the length God will go to let people know they still have a spot on His team no matter how many times they have struck out. I was also embarrassed with the unhealthy relationship I had had with my jacket. Yes, it was an original. Yes, I earned it fair and square. Yes, it cost me more than our bank account wanted to pay, but at the end of the day it was still only a jacket.

Two months later I went to the same restaurant for lunch. I wondered if Mike was working and if he would recognize me. I glanced around the room looking for him, but no sign. Then halfway through my meal I looked up and there he was, staring at me, waving like a politician in a parade again. He walked over to my table and told me, "That day changed my life. The jacket I wanted, but the napkin I needed. It's funny how one note from a stranger helped me find hope again."

I asked him if he still had the jacket, and he said, "Of course! I love that jacket."

9

Stealing Home

Have you ever had those moments you wish you could rewind and relive, hoping for a completely different outcome? You think with time and wisdom in your corner you would have made a better choice. The other day I drove by the school I used to attend when one of those moments snuck up me.

Back then I was doing just fine, working at a factory and making a nice, comfortable living until God invited me to be a pastor. That and being an EMS driver would have been at the bottom of my wish list of career choices. Being a pastor meant wearing a suit and tie, being an EMS driver meant seeing blood ... both gave me the creeps.

After saying no to God and suits for a long time I finally gave up and said yes to to God and maybe to suits. I quit my job, moved back in with my mom, and off to college I went. I was thirty, and the rest of the class was several birthdays behind me. I was sitting in some general-education class all students were forced to take. I was wondering what does this class have to do with being a pastor? It was a history class in which we mostly dialogued and debated the dusty words of smart, dead people.

I don't remember all that was taught in all the classes, but I do remember one of them. We walked into class that day chatting about everything from Freud to Fords and the youthful adventures of the night before. Some of us (like me) were rehearsing speeches as to why our homework was not done. It was a pretty average day.

As our teacher walked in, we scattered to our seats, pretending to be as interested in listening as he was in speaking. He was the type of teacher who let us know he was the scholar and we were the students and we should never confuse the two. He talked to and about women more like they were property than people. He was intentionally arrogant, knowing he gripped our GPAs in his hands and dared anyone to try and take it. The rumors were he would dare students to stand up and prove their points of view only to poke them back into their seats with his thermometer of academic degrees. Most students floated through his class with two objectives: a grade north of a C and Don't rock the boat.

Nothing was different about this class. That was until halfway through without warning he detoured the "dust of the dead" and began to call out women. He started to talk about girls in less than flattering terms. He went on and on about how men are more and women are less, how men are created superior to women, and he had some dead guy's theory to prove it. He was the teacher, we were the students; past classes have taught him we would keep our lips locked, protecting our passing grades. We were forced to be a silent audience to his irrational rant.

Looking across the room, I could see puffs of smoke bellowing out of some of the teenage girls' ears. He went to a place only fools and the arrogant go. He was about seven minutes into his man monologue when he strutted over an ethical line with one silly assumption; with a haughty grin pasted from ear to ear he said, "Oh, one more thing. I want all you girls to know us men are on to your little games you all like to play. You girls, when alone on a date with a guy who is rounding third and you say no, we know you really mean yes. Psychologically, the man knows this and will always attempt to steal home."

He began an awkward chuckle, jiggling the extra thirty pounds draped over his belt that matched his shoes. His laughter was giving everyone a free pass to amen his man message without any academic consequences.

There was no laughter, no amens, only silence. The class looked at each other, hoping someone else would be the hero, but our tongues were collectively frozen with fear. I thought that at the end of his macho tirade we would hear, "I'm only joking; this was just a psychological experiment to see how women would respond to spontaneous criticism from a man." But no, this guy was waiting for us to award him with an Emmy for his one-man, testosterone-injected performance.

Nobody in the class knew what to do. I could sense some of the girls would have easily traded their GPAs for one free kick below his thirty pounds. But before he broke out into an unwanted encore, a young girl four seats to my left began to cry. It was one of those "I don't want to cry but can't help it cries." Within seconds her cry turned into sobs and the sobs turned into wailing.

"What are you crying about?" His callous smirk and cold response had lit her fuse, and we all could see it was a short one.

I have never seen a volcano erupt but was about to.

She wiped away her tears with her sleeve and found courage the class couldn't. With no fear she screamed, "You're wrong! No does not mean yes, no means no!" If it was possible for silence to get quieter, it did. It was one of those rare David-and-Goliath moments when the weak stand up to the schoolyard bully and say, "You ain't takin' my lunch today."

The class gave her a mental standing ovation and five smooth stones to throw. In one corner was an eighteen-year-old girl who had just morphed into a David; in the other, an arrogant Goliath who had spent most of his lonely life hiding behind his framed credentials and brown corduroy blazer with elbow patches. I wasn't sure where the story was going, but my money was on David.

Something happened that caught us all off-guard. She didn't throw a stone. She told a story, her story. The girl invited the whole class into one horrible, dark entry from her journal. Before we could accept or reject her invitation, she dragged the whole class down a flight of stairs into her parents' basement a few years earlier.

They had given her an empty house, proving their trust in their little girl who was growing up. She and her Mr. Right had a fantastic evening, dinner, dancing and what she thought was a movie to top off the perfect date. As the movie ended with credits rolling, this was their cue for a cuddle and a goodnight kiss. He wanted more than a cuddle and a kiss. She politely told him no, it was time to go.

He objected. "If you love me, you'd be willing to go a few bases past first."

Once again she said no and explained, "It's time for you to go."

His voice got louder, informing her he was not going anywhere until he had gotten what he had paid for. He felt two Coney dogs without onions, cheesecake, and flowers from a gas station bought him a home run.

She got up, trying to walk past him only to be shoved to the basement floor. He justified his future sin by telling her it was her fault for wearing her top too low and her skirt too high. He began to scrape off her clothes like paint from an old building.

She screamed at him, "No! Stop! Stop!" but he had already determined he was going to steal home. She shouted out toward heaven for help only to hear the sound of his panting and God's silence. She pleaded with angels to get this devil off her.

To silence her screams he punched her in the jaw and told her to shut up. He continued to force his will at the cost of hers. She ran out of help and hope and gave up, letting him score.

When he crossed over home plate he reminded her, "Ya know, it didn't have to be this way. If you would have just given me what I wanted, none of this would have happened." He left her bruised and lying in a puddle of blood at home plate.

She pondered, "I don't know what hell looks like but I do know what it smells like: two Coney dogs without onions."

The whole class sat speechless after being forced to eavesdrop on her unlocked journal. Some girls in the class were crying with and for her. The entry was meant more for a shrink than for students. I will swear on a stack of Bibles that when she had woken up that morning she'd never thought the ink of her journal would spill all over a class of strangers. When she was done sharing his sin and her shame, we didn't know if we should have called the police or a priest. We did neither.

She looked right in the tearless eyes of the teacher and asked one question. "So tell me, when I said no that night, do you think I meant yes? Do you think he was right that I owed him a home run in exchange for Coney dogs? Every day of my life I wake up and go to bed wondering what I could have done different that night. Every time a guy looks at me, I wonder if he likes me or just wants to round the bases. This may be some college experiment to you, but to me it's not funny."

The teacher for the first time personally saw the welts his careless words had caused. He tried to fumble out a halfhearted apology. "I'm, ahh, well, umm, that's not what I meant." You could tell Goliath was stunned by her story, but it was obvious the apology thing was new to him.

We all prayed for the bell to ring because nobody knew the closing lines to this drama. The bell finally rang, putting a period on the life lesson we had witnessed. When we left, no one was talking about Freud, Fords, or late assignments. No one said anything to the teacher, the girl, or each other. We all stood up, grabbed our books, and went to our next class, changed but not knowing if it was for the better or worse.

That is the day I wish I could rewind and relive. I justified my silence by convincing myself that I was brand new at this Jesus stuff, that God wouldn't expect a newbie like me to take on such a major problem. I justified my silence by assuming someone else should have spoken up, someone smarter than a factory rat like me. I justified my silence by thinking, What if he flunks me for speaking up and out? Our silence forced her to unlock a journal with words written but never meant to be read out loud.

It's been decades since that class. I don't remember what her name was or what she was wearing, but I do remember her journal entry that day. I wonder how many times she has replayed that professor's sloppy comments and pondered, Maybe he was right. Maybe I did deserve it. I wonder if she's married with kids of her own. I wonder if she forbids her daughter to be alone with a boy till she's thirty-five. I wonder if her husband questions why she sometime cries after making love. I wonder if she ever ate a Coney Island again.

But most of all I wonder what God would have done if I had spoken up. I have thought over and over again what I would have said or done different on that day. I told a buddy of mine over lunch about this twenty-year-old diary dilemma.

In between bites of his burger he said something that seemed to make no sense.

"Tell her now."

"Maybe you didn't catch the fact that one, this happened over twenty years ago, and two, you can't change the past."

Not fazed by my left-brain logic, he said, "Do you think she's the only girl in the world that has happened to? Don't you think by writing what you wish you had done may help someone else know what to do in the same situation? I don't know … just a thought." He went back to disposing his burger. I thought, Maybe he's right.

So here is what I wish I would have done if I could have gotten a mulligan on that day over twenty years ago:

I'm not sure what your name is, but first of all I want to say I'm sorry. I will not write you this letter telling you I know what it's like to have someone steal home. I will not pull out my black Bible and preach to you about high skirts and low tops. I was young once and have enough skeletons in my closet to start a museum. I too have a journal I would rather burn than blab out loud. I'm sorry none of us did anything that day. No, I'm sorry I did nothing that day. I was a brand-new Christian at the time. I felt your battle that day was bigger than my bullets. I thought God used new Christians only for simple stuff like praying before meals and passing out bulletins on Sunday mornings. But to have advice on stealing home? That was a real preacher's job.

Having had twenty years to think about it, I wish I had asked your name. I wish I had cried with you or at least for you. I wish I had invited you to my church. It was not a perfect church, but they helped me get through a few of my dark entries. I wish I had prayed with you or at least for you that day. I wish I had worried more about you than my stupid GPA. I wish I had had the courage to stand up to a person who acted more like a junior high bully than a college professor.

I'm sorry for what you went through that night. I don't have any magic wand to make your entry disappear. None of us has big enough erasers to blot out the sins of others in our journals. I know none of us was in the basement to stop it, but we could have said something, anything, in that class to help. I was a poor example of God's mercy and grace that day.

You impressed me that day, not that you twirled your sling and stone and cold-cocked Goliath but that you opened up your journal and shared your story with a class full of timid mutes. You were not just sticking up for you but for every young girl who has lost her innocence by force. All our lives were moved by your courage that day; sorry it took me over twenty years to tell you.

My hope is that by writing this story, your story, someone will realize none of us can change the past but with small acts of compassion we can help heal the future. Maybe someone will read this and realize no means no. Maybe someone will read this and at the end of the movie go home instead. Who knows? Maybe someone will read this and realize stealing home fits better on a ball field than in a basement.

Maybe she stayed single and hates all men. Who knows? Maybe she married the boy in the basement and they have three kids and vacation in the Gulf of Mexico. Maybe the teacher went home, had a beer, and told his wife about the overreaction of one of his students that day. Maybe he realized he had committed an error and had apologized the next day.

The boy in the basement and that corduroy Casanova of a teacher are easy targets to hurl stones at. But I have learned over the past twenty years, having heard this girl's story dozens of times, the people who throw the most stones are usually the people who have been hit by the most stones. This in no way excuses what they did, but it does help explain it.

All I know is that you can't rewind time whether you are a victim or a villain. You can't go back and fix twenty-year-old mistakes, but you can do the right thing today. That way, twenty years from now you won't have to write a story like this one.

10

The Couch

It was two o'clock in the morning, and I couldn't sleep. If you asked anyone close to me, that was nothing new; I have a poor habit of tinkering with things only God can fix. I stumbled downstairs to our worn, brown leatherish couch to watch reruns of ESPN sports center. That night it was storming on the outside and on the inside. Outside the thunder was loud and the lightning was sneaking in through the half-closed curtains. Inside, I was rewinding my day of the things I should have or could have done better. Families struggling to make ends meet … A friend's divorce that was an inch away … The homeless scraping for their next meal … An alcoholic who thought he'd received his healing only to only find himself staring at the bottom of a bottle … again.

Somewhere in the middle of attempting to solve all God's problems I heard a noise. It was not the sound of thunder but the sound of my young daughter Morgan plopping down the steps.

"What's up, buddy?"

"Dad, I'm scared of the storm and can't sleep. Can I sit on the couch with you?" She crawled up on the couch, and I flipped the station to watch a rerun of her favorite show, "Diners, Drive-Ins, and Dives." With each beat of the thunder she burrowed closer and closer to me until there was no space between us. I said, "Morgan, you can't get any closer."

"But I can try."

I reached back into my paternal card catalogue of wisdom for a few words of comfort and remembered what I used to tell her when she was five.

"Morgan, nothing will happen to you as long as you're with daddy." That line had always worked in the past and seemed to fit nicely in between the thunder and lightning exhibition.

Without any hesitation she responded, "Dad, you can't promise me that, right? Just because I'm sitting next to you doesn't mean bad things can't happen."

It was a moment she was right but wished she were wrong.

I like to think I'm in control and nothing bad will happen on my watch. But many storms have proven Morgan right and me wrong considering the devastation they can leave behind to good people.

Though she was only ten, she'd heard enough of my sermons to know bad things do happen to good people. Storms are not very selective as to whose lives they tip over. I knew where my daughter's fear had gotten its start. We had lived in a manufactured home and had seen what storms can do to them on the news. We both remember watching the news during a terrible storm when the weatherman said, "If you live in a mobile home you have a better chance of living if you go and lie in your front yard." Yes, that's what he said, and no, that didn't comfort either of us.

I assured her, "You're right, Morgan. I can't promise you nothing bad will happen. But I can promise you I will sit on the couch with you until the storm is over." Thankfully that worked; calmly she laid her head on my chest, fell asleep, and drooled all over my shirt.

It's funny how in the middle of the storm, in the middle of her fear, I wished I could take a hammer and smash to pieces time and stay camped on the couch; I didn't want that moment to end. It was one of those selfish father moments I felt I really needed. I had made a lot of mistakes by that time, but I thought whatever the definition of a "good father" is, that night I fit it.

I felt a bit guilty, however, for even thinking such an odd thought. Why would I want to stop time here? Who in their right minds wants life to stop smack-dab in the middle of a storm? Why not stop time when she burbled Da-Da for first time? Why not stop time at her first steps? Why was I so at peace in the middle of her storm? It just seems like a strange place to stop time.

Maybe it was because I knew that that moment would evaporate into a memory in the blink of an eye. I knew how fast time travels with or without my permission. I knew somewhere there's some guy not worthy of my approval waiting to take my place on the couch. I knew there was some guy who was going to tell her he loved her more than I do, and no matter how hard I tried to convince her it was a lie she would believe it. I knew there was some guy who would come and ask me if he could steal my daughter from me. After I'd accidently kick him in the shin, sock him in the gut, and twisted his hat around the right way, I'd reluctantly say yes. Well, maybe I'd say yes, no guarantees. I also knew there was another guy who would be sitting on an empty couch in the middle of a storm wishing for this moment to magically appear just one more time. A moment when he felt he was a good dad.

The loud racket and light show moved on to perform for a different city. I gently tapped her on the shoulder. "Honey, the storm's over."

She quietly yawned. "Thanks Dad, good night."

That night I wasn't sure who needed whom the most. So I willingly gave the world back to God and headed upstairs to bed. I didn't solve all the world's problems that night, but for a few minutes I had forgotten all of mine.

At times I wish I were more like Morgan. She has this truth thing going on in her life. With her you seldom have to guess what she's feeling because she will just blurt it out. When she's happy she says she's happy. When she's hungry she'll ask for food over and over and over again. As a small child, she would time her visit with all our neighbors so she could invade their breakfasts, lunches, and dinners by asking, "Hey, do you have some food I can eat?" Or nights like that night when she's frightened and honestly says, "Dad, I'm scared," and expects me to do something to make her not scared. She knows I will do anything I can to calm her down. She has zero fear I will reject her plea for a place on the couch. She thinks, "Hey, you're my dad! You better protect me, because that's your job."

God so wants us to run to Him like Morgan ran to me at the first drop of rain. Yet too many people when going through storms run away from God, not to Him. They feel He is too busy tinkering with all the world's big storms in faraway countries. They feel they are bugging Him and are not good enough to drool on His chest. They are scared to cry out to Him with the truth of Morgan and say, "Daddy, I'm scared. Can I sit next to you on the couch until the storm passes?" They fear He is going to be some wicked father barking back, "Get back to bed you big baby!"

This is not the picture the Bible paints of God; God wants us to cry out to him. He wants us to run to Him in our storms of life no matter whose fault they are. He wants us to be truthful and admit we are scared and tell Him to move over and then hop up on the couch with Him.

If you have any doubts about His love, just read Luke fifteen. It's one of my favorite stories in the Bible. It's about a boy who decided he didn't need his dad or his couch anymore because he was a man. He flew off to New York City to do, well, whatever boys who think they're men do. But as soon as his cash was gone and the storm hit, he got scared; he decided to see if his old man would take him back.

When he got home he had this "I'm sorry" speech memorized. He mentally practiced every line, planning to deliver it when he walked up to his father: "Dad, it's all my fault … Dad, I was so stupid to leave you and Mom … Dad, I know you don't have to, but do you think maybe you could, um, ah, forgive me?"

But his dad never let him speak; he was so excited to see his boy walking up the steps that he grabbed his soaking wet son, hugging and kissing the fear out of him. Not once did the dad say, "I told you this was going to happen! Now get back upstairs you big baby. You're grounded!"

None of that happened because he was just so glad to have his son back on the couch again that the boy didn't get to recite his speech.

I have lost count of how many times I have run from God instead of to Him in my storms. You would think after doing this Jesus thing for many years and getting soaked in hundreds of storms I would have learned by now, but I still think I can sit on the couch only if I have it all together. Frankly, there are times I'm scared to death by what life throws at me and yet I stand out in rain, wishing I were on the couch, drooling on my Father's chest, but fear of my past mistakes keeps me off the couch and in the storm.

That night I remembered looking down at my daughter as she was snoring in complete peace, not because the storms had stopped but because she was with me. How would the story have read if when my daughter came downstairs crying for comfort I had said, "Go back to bed you big sissy. You're ten! Grow up and act your age."

Knowing my daughter, she would have said, "But Dad, I'm scared."

If I had responded that way, she would have gone upstairs and covered her head with her blankets and cried herself to sleep. God loves to hear our feet tromping down the stairs telling Him we are scared. He will stop tinkering with the world and watch "Diners, Drive-Ins, and Dives" with us until the storm is over.

I think people scared of storms are tired of the church telling them, "Come to Jesus and all your storms will be over." Nobody gets through life without getting soaked by a few of its storms. Morgan was right: we can't promise anybody storms will never cause us hurt. I, like you, wonder at times why God doesn't just stop the storms, but that question will have to be addressed in heaven or by someone much smarter than me. All I know is I want to be more like Morgan and know that when the storms of life hit there will always be a place for me on my Father's couch. We all need someone not to promise we will never go through storms but to promise we will never go through them alone.

Go ahead, tell Him your greatest fears, tell Him what you're scared of; He won't kick you in the shin, sock you in the gut, or tell you to turn your hat around. He will scooch over and make room for you on His couch.

11

Hating Dead People

I was invited to preach a revival for a small church in a small town. It's a place whose team colors are John Deere green and yellow. Carhartt's, Red Wing boots, and denim overalls are considered Sunday best. If you saw people who looked like they were hiding golf balls in their cheeks, one spit would tell you they were not. All the waitresses in town call everyone sweetheart or honey. I was asked to come and preach a little new life into a few old saints; the pastor gave me four days to raise the dead. The average age was, well, let's just say most of them could get their coffee discounted at McDonald's.

When I arrived at the church, the people were, as I expected, country folk grateful to be able to rent a new preacher for a few days. People brought me homemade pies, cakes, cookies, and even a bag of potatoes (from a garden) as gifts each night before I spoke. People were very eager and open to share their stories of life and loss. Each night I was corralled by broken people, all hoping and praying I was the shortcut to their healing.

It was a great hand full of nights during which I served a platter of hope and encouragement each night. I enjoyed being smothered with their small-town love and treats.

Then it was the last night. By that time I knew a few of the folks by their first names, and they all knew mine. But I was a bit tired and really missing my wife and kids.

I stood at the back door of the church, shaking hands probably more like a politician than a pastor. People were telling me what a difference the week had made in their lives. Someone slipped a folded twenty into my hands for gas on the way home. Someone else passed on a parting gift for my wife and kids for letting them borrow me for a few days.

The service was about to start, so I grabbed my Bible and headed to the pulpit. As I was walking toward the front of the church, I felt a hand grab mine. I turned to see what was going on. This short, round woman was looking up at me and asking if we could talk. I tried to sneak a glance at the clock in the front of the church to see how to respond. The entire flock was patiently sitting in the pews, waiting to be fed in a few seconds.

Before I could answer, she vomited her past and pain all over me. There were no pies, cookies, or potatoes, just anger ... lots and lots of anger. She told me she hated her husband. She yelled it out as if she were on the "Dr. Phil" show.

"My husband molested my young daughter. My daughter was messed up. Our marriage was messed up, and I'm messed up. Do you know what it's like waking up every day being messed up? Every day I looked at her I hated him more. I just thought he was getting up in the middle of the night to go the bathroom. I hate him! I should have noticed, but who thinks the man you sleep with is, well, you know?

"Then out of guilt I started to blame myself for not seeing the signs. I should have protected her and I didn't. I never would have suspected he would do something like this. I live with this pile of guilt like an unwanted roommate every day of my life. I spend almost every day of my life pretending I'm alright, and I'm tired of lying and living. You're a preacher—tell me what to do! Tell me why the God you show off each night here would allow a grown man to do what he did to a little girl, especially when she is his own. Tell me how I can fix this mess. I can't keep living this way. I want to be strong for my daughter, but I'm so weak and ready to simply give up."

The woman started to cry, still clutching my hand with more hate than hope. I saw that my three great sermons on hope had not been able to penetrate her heart of stone. I was caught off-guard; this was so not what I had expected for the last night. I thought after the service we would all hug, and they would tell me what a great preacher I was and that they wanted to book me for next year's revival. I looked down at my sermon notes peeking out of my Bible and I knew I was in trouble. I had no magic pill in my notes to heal a heart that broken. I'd been doing this preaching thing long enough to know that if this woman did not forgive him she would have to serve a life of hard time and hate with no chance of parole. I knew the right words but didn't have the guts to share them. Forgiveness is not as easy as many preachers make it sound.

I looked out at the sheep in the pews; they were getting restless because it was past their feeding time. People were looking at their watches, wanting to get their money's worth of a rented preacher. They'd paid for four nights, and they wanted four nights … that was just good stewardship of God's money. Something inside me wanted to scrap the whole service and sermon that night. I remembered the passage in Luke in which Jesus left the ninety-nine for the one. I wanted to do that, but my fear of the flock and what they would say kept that beautiful red verse safely tucked inside my Bible.

I sent a six-word prayer her way. "God, please heal her heart, amen."

She walked away and gave me an obligated thank you. I think we both resolved that this might have been a hurt too big for even God to heal. Before you go off scolding me that "God can do all things," I will agree with you in my head but sadly not always in my heart. Sometimes people's problems seem so much bigger than God's solutions.

She gradually melted into the back pew on the left side of the church. I slowly walked to the front of the church to preach. I had opened each night with something funny just to warm up the crowd, but I was standing behind the pulpit, staring at that woman in the back, and realizing no joke in Vegas could heal what was broken that night. I was staring at my open Bible and a yellow legal pad tattooed with religious black ink. I wasn't saying a word. People were looking at me, wondering why the preacher wasn't preaching.

I cautiously began to speak not from my head but from my heart. I had no points, poems, or jokes, just a tangled tongue that was trying to straighten out a tangled woman. I seldom ever preach at a person, trying to fix him or her from the pulpit, but I made an exception that night. I rambled out words of hope more like a father to a daughter than a pastor to a parishioner. I had no clue what I said that night, but I do know who I said it to. I told her, "God still loves you and weeps when you weep." I flipped those words a dozen ways that night and just let the ninety-nine listen in on the one-on-one sermon.

After several minutes of trying to speak for God, I closed with a short prayer, trying not to embarrass her. "God, I pray you will bring hope to the hopeless. I pray you would help heal all those who are hurting tonight, amen." I felt so inadequate that night; I just wanted to sneak out the back door and go home. I felt I had failed God, this woman, and the church that night. I had failed God for not having the courage to rescue the one, I had failed the woman for not having a shortcut to her healing, and I had failed the church for being more concerned with my notes than their hurts. For three days I had boasted of the power of God, yet I felt so impotent standing alone behind that pulpit. Everybody was staring at me and not the clocks. None of us knew what to do next.

Then I saw a hand raised slowly from the back, left-hand side of the church. In the back row the tormented woman had her hand up, wanting to talk. Here we go, I thought. She's going to haul out our private conversation in front of the whole church. I didn't know if her daughter was there. For all I knew, her husband could have been parked on the right side of the church and she was going to rat him out in front of God and the packed pews.

I had no option but to let her speak. I nodded in her direction. It was like lighting a fuse, giving her permission to explode.

"It worked!" She wildly yelled.

"What worked?" I played along.

"It worked! It worked! Your prayer, it worked!"

I was embarrassed when I said out loud what I should have kept silent. I asked, "Ahh, what prayer?"

"Remember when you prayed with me just before the service? 'God, please heal her heart, amen'?"

I'd been in such a hurry to preach and had felt the pressure to be on time that I had forgotten what I'd prayed.

She spoke with the voice of an angel. "I'm free, I'm free! Somewhere in the middle of all your talking tonight, I felt like God told me, If you forgive your husband, I will heal you. I got so spitting mad at God, telling Him, 'But God, my husband is dead, been dead for five years.' I don't know how to unhate a dead person. How can I forgive a dead person? Then I figured, what do I have to lose except the hate, guilt, and shame? So I whispered a silent prayer half as long as yours, 'I forgive him.' As soon as those words reached heaven, I was free. So you see, pastor, God did answer your prayer for me."

It's sad to say, but I'm not sure if she or I was more surprised at her newfound freedom. So many people regularly pelt me with problems so much bigger than my degree. There are times I pray feeling all heaven is on my side, feeling I can whip the world with one hand tied behind my back. But many times I pray dry, boring, selfish, routine prayers just because that's what pastors do. This bothers me about myself. I want every prayer I pray to be packed with dynamite, but many times they feel like they're duds.

But not that night; God taught us both that the power of prayer is not in the arrangement of clever Christian clichés. It's not in titles, sermons, education, wealth, or poverty; the power is in the person we pray to. A desperate woman needed God more than she needed me or my sermon that night. She needed a prayer even if it was short and rushed. I'm so glad God takes prayer so much more seriously than do the flimsy people who pray them.

On my long drive home to my family that night, I realized how much God is in love with broken people. I was thinking how many people in this world hate dead people. People who still wear the scars of being sucker punched by family, friends, and strangers who took their "I'm sorry" to the grave with them.

For five years a woman had been stomping and spitting on a dead man's grave, trying to dig up six words: "I'm sorry, will you forgive me?" Here's the weird thing about forgiveness: it has this backward way of healing us more than the other person. I don't think anyone can forgive and forget. I don't think what that man did to his daughter was right. Saying I'm sorry is not a get out of jail free card. But I do believe that with God's grace we can forgive and be free. Forgiving is not about letting someone off the hook; it's about letting ourselves off the hook. She never got her six words; she got something far better. And she got back her freedom, freedom from hating a dead person. Today is always better than tomorrow to give and receive forgiveness.

12

Love Wins

Back in the day, a friend and I went to one of those bar-restaurant joints for a night of chatter, chow, and Kool and the Gang. We were two young guys holding up a wall when we noticed a brawny, bald man staring at us. Do I know this guy? I asked myself. Because if I do, by his look I don't think we're friends. After a few minutes it became clear that Buddy was the target of his evil eye, not me. It's not like Buddy and I were angels, but hey, we'd just walked into the place. We glanced at each other and silently agreed we had no clue whom the mystery madman was.

Buddy had picked up on it before I had. "Just let it go, Dennis."

"Let what go?"

"Just let it go." Buddy had been down this dirt road many times. "I think he doesn't like black people." He was unfortunately used to the ignorant stares and racial mumblings. This was not the first time this drama had acted itself out in our youthful adventures.

I witnessed times when white people just walked up, pushed, and provoked him, looking for a fight. Most of the time he did very well, responding with grace, living up to his nickname, Buddy. He had taken heat from whites and blacks for being too white or too black. What I most respected about Buddy was that he never wanted to be defined solely by the color of his skin. He had a winsome personality that would teach anyone paying attention how to get along with difficult people. To me he was a walking billboard for the Golden Rule: do to others as you would have them do to you. Buddy would politely refuse any halo that would come his way, just quoting, "That's what my dad always taught me."

I never understood what this was like until I went over to East Lansing for an event Magic Johnson was hosting. At the time he was just graduating from Michigan State, but the whole world knew he was going to be a star. I walked into the place and immediately realized I was one of the few whites in the place. It took only a second to think of Buddy and what he observed every day. When walking around, for the first time I was conscious of my color. I'd never been conscious of my color. It was not that I didn't know I was white; I'd just never been forced to think about it in public. As I strolled through the place, some people were very nice and struck up conversations. Others pushed and provoked, looking for a response. I thought, "What have I done except just walk in the door?" It was the same scene Buddy was in that night.

I was watching this guy get closer and closer to Buddy, wondering what would happen. One of him, two of us; I wasn't good at math, but that sounded like good odds. If this guy makes a move, I thought, we should be able to wrestle him to the ground and sit on him until the police show up.

Then he began with some slight taunting that quickly ratcheted up to racial slurs. He was as annoying as a mosquito juiced up on Red Bull. He kept trying to bait Buddy into a fight. I was watching and waiting for Buddy to go off on him. I was thinking, I know you're a nice guy and all that Golden Rule stuff your dad taught you, but this bully has a beating coming to him. All Buddy did was stare straight ahead without looking at him and absorbed every hateful word heaved his way.

Then he made a move toward Buddy. Here we go, I thought. It's on.

But what happened that next moment has stayed with me for twenty-five years. The guy, the mean, nasty, good-for-nothing, hate-heaving guy reached out his hand. Wait a minute. What's he doing? Why is he reaching out his hand? Then Buddy reached out his hand, knowing exactly what was happening. He was making peace; the hate was turning into a handshake.

He told Buddy, "I like you. You're a good guy," and bought him a soda (okay, maybe not a soda). The two of them stood there swapping stories.

What just happened? This is not the ending I expected or anticipated.

I can tell you now what I didn't know then. Love won. Love may have not won the night before or the night after, but that night love won. Buddy could have turned him into the owner. He could have walked out. He could have preached a sermon on racism. He could have justified rifling back a few ethnic zingers. He could have slugged the guy right in his chops (my personal favorite), but instead he chose to fight with the most powerful word in the world, "love."

Who would have thought that twenty-five years later I would be a pastor and Buddy would be our church bouncer, I mean, greeter? Buddy is still pretty green in his faith. He's never read any books or taken any classes on how to be a holy greeter, and I have no plans of corrupting him by sending him to one.

Buddy has a gift that can't be taught or bought. He has the gift of love. He knows what it's like to be on the receiving end of people's prejudices. Buddy has accepted his role as ambassador, the whole box of crayons, not just those who look like him.

When you come to our church you will have to duck and dodge rather quickly to escape Buddy's 270-pound bear hug. Some have tried but few have succeeded.

Honestly, if I miss a week preaching, people will say, "Oh, Dennis, how was your little break?" But if Buddy is ten minutes late, our folks are calling out the National Guard. I'm sure some people walk in thinking they aren't used to receiving a hug from a large black man, but three weeks later there's Buddy, hugging them again, and two weeks after that they're upset if they don't get their Buddy hug.

How does he do it? Buddy knows what so many church people have forgotten. Whether they're in restaurants or churches, people are looking for love. Somewhere between when folks get their first hug until their most recent they stop looking at Buddy as a big, black man who hugs. They look at him as a man who freely gives out God's love, one hug at a time, to anyone who's willing to accept them.

That night, love won.

13
People Like Me

After miles and miles of chasing a prodigal friend, I was bent over, huffing and puffing with exhaustion. I was too old, and he was too young for me to keep up with. He'd made it very clear he wanted nothing to do with me or my religion. It seemed the more I chased him, the further he drifted from God. He would drop in the church every now and then just to get his wife off his back. I told God and him I'd be there waiting with open arms when he was ready to come back to church without being dragged.

After piles and piles of prayers petitioning heaven on his behalf, he finally called. In a very tranquil voice he invited me to meet him at the church. I could not disguise my excitement. I shouted, "Man, I've been waiting years for this call."

"Okay, see ya in few," he said.

I began to dance with the angels in heaven over one lost sinner coming home (or at least coming to church). I praised God for hearing and finally answering my prayers. I sprinted over to the church, waiting to make good on my welcome-home hug. If I'd had time I would have made one of those welcome-home banners and draped it from the steeple.

He slowly meandered up the driveway to the church. I opened the door as wide as my arms. I went to hug him, but he ducked under my arms and marched to the front of the church. His intentional detour around my hug seemed a bit odd, but my enthusiasm blurred out my normal instincts. I followed him in and parked right next to him. I was curious as to what had turned his heart toward heaven and home. He sat there, silently staring at the cross in the front of the church. I thought maybe he was quietly praising God for saving him; maybe he was tossing up a few prayers heaven's way, thanking God for what an awesome pastor I was. So we sat in silence.

But five minutes of silence were too much for my tongue, so I started snooping as to what had brought this black sheep back to the flock. I punctured the hush with one innocent question, "What brought you back to God?" He didn't respond. So I quickly repeated, "What brought you home?"

He looked at me and raised his voice to decibels that would shatter stained glass, belting out, "The hell with God! You can keep Him! I don't want anything to do with Him anymore. I don't care if He hears me swearing in church. It doesn't matter because He's dumped me. He doesn't pay much attention to people like me. This God-and-Jesus stuff is a bunch of crap!" (Or something like that.)

Well, that explained the detour around my welcome-home hug.

"You asked me what brought me home? This isn't home. This place is more like hell than home. To come to church and not see or feel God—isn't that what hell is? A place without God? Every place I go lately is a place without God. So I guess I have a few questions for you. Why does God talk to you and not to me? Why does God love people like you and not people like me?"

His was not some spontaneous, sacred ambush. I could tell his lines had been well rehearsed. I tried to cross-examine him, "What do you mean, people like you?" Once again, silence filled up the sanctuary. His eyes pivoted back to the cross. I tried to nudge a little Jesus his way, reminding him, "Jesus says He loves everybody."

"Yeah, well, then I'm the exception."

"Why would you be the exception?"

He said out loud what the whole town had whispered privately. "I have a mental illness. I have prayed to your God to fix me, and He didn't, or worse yet wouldn't. The few times my wife made me come to church you preach warm, fuzzy sermons telling us all how good God is and how He wants to answer our prayers. You spit out some verse that says 'ask anything in My name and you shall receive it.' If that's true, tell me why God won't answer my prayers."

He reminisced. "I sat in your church one Sunday and heard this old lady pray for a parking space at the mall, and she got it. She went on and on about how good God was to open up a spot near the front of the mall. Heck, she was almost crying over a parking spot that magically appeared. Does she have any idea how that sounds to people like me? My knuckles are bloody from knocking on heaven's door, not for a parking spot but for a new mind. I really did try to pray God would heal my mind and shoo the voices away. I don't know how to pray as well as you, but I did try. But as you can tell, after years and years of praying, my mind is getting worse, not better. What do you want me to do? This is embarrassing. Am I supposed to act like it doesn't hurt when people mock me with their laughter? I see the way my wife looks at me with more pity than love. I think sometimes she stays with me only because it wouldn't look good on her future dating résumé to divorce a person like me. You know what it's like to have to nod your head up and down, pretending you understand the simplest of conversations? You know what it's like to drive to the grocery store and not know how to find your way back home? Sometimes I sit in the parking lot for hours because I'm too embarrassed to call my wife and ask for directions … again.

"Am I supposed to hear the voices taunting me daily to take my life? Every day I wake up and feel the world would be a much better place without people like me. How long am I supposed to keep holding on to a God who has let go of me? Some days I think God made a cruel mistake when He made people like me. I dream that maybe when God's not so busy in third world countries He could fix the mental defect that came as standard equipment at my birth. But I wake up like I always wake up, hearing every hissing voice but His. When you preach that 'Jesus loves us' stuff each week, forgive me for not buying the manure you're selling. You may be able to get 'fixed' people to buy a few bags, but people like me? Sorry. So, like I said, God? Well, He can just go to hell. Then maybe I can hear and see Him because that's where I live every day."

I was tripping over my laces, stumbling for a comeback, a verse, a theological response, but nothing seemed right but silence. A few minutes earlier his silence had bullied my big mouth wide open, but right then my ignorance was keeping it shut.

His head collapsed into his hands, and he started mumbling what he always mumbled, "What's wrong with me? Why won't God fix me?" He was puzzled why God would allow one baby to be born normal and another like him. Why would God clear a parking spot but not clear his mind?

Like so many other lost sheep wandering around in the dark, he felt God loved "fixed" people but not broken people like him. I'd heard that lie repeated a thousand times over in my brief pastoral career. I've said it myself more times than I'm willing to admit. Satan has used the same ol' stale trick from the beginning of time; he baits us into believing we have done something so bad, or something has been done to us, to disqualify us from His love. He notifies us we are too messed up, too far gone, and too broke to ever be loved. Just look around you and see the faces of those who have swallowed the bait.

A thirteen-year-old girl gets pregnant at her first junior high dance, and her expanding belly tattles on her more and more each day. She thinks God doesn't love people like me.

A women flirting with fifty has already vowed "I do" and "I don't" to five men only to be sleeping alone again. She thinks God doesn't love people like me.

A father pounces on his kid like a piñata just like his ol' man had pounced on him. He looks in the mirror each morning, hating himself more and more. He thinks God doesn't love people like me.

A Vietnam vet drinks every day and night, hoping to drown out the screams of those his bullets had buried. He was welcomed home with protestors' homemade signs reading "Child Killers." He thinks God doesn't love people like me.

A man has spent more years in prison than out of it. He is free now, but all people see is his past. He thinks God doesn't love people like me.

A mom takes a catnap on a Sunday afternoon and her two-year-old stumbles into the pool and drowns. She can't sleep without pills and nightmares. She thinks God doesn't love people like me.

A pastor who had a one-night stand with his secretary lost his flock, family, and faith in the back of a Dodge in the church parking lot. He thinks God doesn't love people like me.

Or a black sheep sitting in the right place in his wrong mind, a guy who wakes up every day feeling he's a neon billboard advertising one of God's biggest mistakes. He, like all the others, feels the world would be a much better place without people like him.

Wow, had I ever misread this welcome-home party. I felt foolish. I must admit I was buying a little of what he was selling. Why was I born whole and he was born broke? Why can I find my way home from the store without calling for directions? Why does my wife love me more than she pities me?

We both were stuck in sacred silence, staring at the cross. I took a chance telling him one more time, "God does love people like you and me." It was not that I thought it was the right thing to say but rather the only thing. We all have times in our lives when we are walking billboards for what we are not. I shared, "I don't think I know why we are born the way we are born. I'm so sorry you can't hear God's voice. I'm sorry you feel this world would be a better place without people like you. Every day people with smart, fully functioning minds jump off bridges, pull triggers, and swallow pills, all feeling the world would be a better place without them. You could have jumped, pulled, and swallowed, but you didn't. Why did you call me to meet at the church? It had to be more than telling God where to go. You could have done that from home. Why are you here?"

He paused and said, "I'm here because I forgot what God's voice sounded like. I knew when I came here, even after saying words that fit more in a pub than in a pew, you would still tell me God loves me. You always tell me God loves me even when I'm mad at Him and you. I had two choices today, go to the bridge or go to the church. Today I picked the church."

He leaned over and gave me the long overdue hug he had avoided on the way in. I wanted to tell him so much more, but that day "Jesus loves people like you" was enough. He got up and walked out the same but different. I don't know if the angels where dancing or crying, but I do know he had heard my voice and thought it was God's.

I have gone through boxes of shoes sprinting after people who don't want to be caught. They have always been too fast for my faith. I do believe prayer has the power to steer a prodigal in the right direction, but it can't make them walk in it. Every day people wake up telling God where to go and that they are tired of being His billboard for brokenness. Every day people hear voices telling them this world would be better without them. What they don't need is one more voice pointing at their billboards telling them what's wrong. Sometimes the best we can do is stand at open doors with open arms and wait for prodigals to come home.

It was pretty cool. He started coming to church a few times a month without being blasted with guilt from his wife. He never barked out a hallelujah, amen, or became a member. He never told the people, me, or God where to go, so that was a step in the right direction. Every now and then I saw something that resembled the curve of a smile, but he would adamantly deny it. I'm not sure God answered my prayers that day, but I do know He answered his. He just wanted to hear what all lost sheep want to hear, "Jesus loves people like you no matter what your billboards says."

14

Pink High-Tops

My life was falling apart faster than my anorexic faith could fix it. The more toys I bought, the emptier I felt. The more money I made, the more I wasted. I remembered driving around in a bright red Porsche, alone, thinking something was wrong with this picture. How can I have so much stuff and still feel so empty? It seems everything I do to make myself happy does the opposite. I'm lonely, single, and wishing I weren't either. I am lost without a map or a next move. I can't keep driving down this same road, but I'm too scared to try another.

At the same time my parents and God were tag teaming up on me to try church one more time. It had been years since I had darkened the doors of a church. I exited the church at eighteen not expecting to ever go back. I balked at their requests, being that I had grown up in the church and was not fond of my boring experiences. My faded, childhood memories brought back more of a yawn than a hallelujah. I felt like a flop. Why would I want to go to church to have some preacher poke his bony finger at the error of my ways?

One Sunday I woke up and said more out of desperation than desire, "This is the day I go back to church." After years of playing my award-winning role as the prodigal, I didn't know how I would be received. I thought church was just for nice people with nice clothes. I had no church clothes and was not real nice at the time.

I sifted through my closet, which looked and smelled like a gym locker, one of the few perks of being single. I was trying to find some outfit that would not make me look like the sinner I was. I tried on several things to try to blend in with the believers; I even pondered wearing my one funeral suit, but every time I looked in the mirror I said to myself, This isn't me. Why am I trying to impress people I don't know? So I made the call. I would dress the way I dressed when going to bars. I was hoping the church in my absence had relaxed a bit on the dress code. I didn't like the way I felt. I had never spent that much time and effort on what I would wear. I just wanted to fit in with the crowd. I was about to learn that it's hard for a black sheep to hide in a white flock.

The ensemble I chose was a short-sleeved shirt, a pair of shorts, and pink high-top Converse tennis shoes. I was addicted to Chuck Taylors back in the day. I had gone to New York City and found this gem of a store near Times Square that sold Converses in every color of the rainbow and dozens more. To fill my fix, I bought the whole rainbow.

I was scared to death to walk into church after years of my self-enforced sin sabbatical. I was scared God would let the skeletons out of my closet in front of the nice church folks. I was scared about what people might say to me. I was scared someone would say, "Sorry, you're too far gone for God." My stomach was tumbling with fear. Right about then all I wanted to do was go out to breakfast, read the paper, and postpone my church reunion, let's say, oh, for about thirty years.

I sat in my sports car outside church, trying to persuade myself this Jesus thing was a good idea. Well, I decided to cash in on my promise to myself. I tiptoed in the doors, feeling every person in the joint was staring at me. I somehow felt the Devil had e-mailed them all my sins and they couldn't wait to post them on the bulletin board.

Once inside, I didn't know "where to go" and was frightened to ask the question considering my past. So I just followed a herd of nice-looking sheep into a big room packed with pews. Not a lot of people were saying anything to me, but by their glances at my pink Chuck Taylors I was feeling a bit judged. To be fair, it probably had more to do with my fear than their stares.

I was mentally repeating, Okay, you can do this, you can do this. Just keep your mouth shut and smile like you've been here before.

My plan was working to perfection until I bumped into the church bouncer, or should I say she bumped into me. She was all of eighty-three pounds and towered at four feet plus a few inches. She looked old and mean. She dressed like she had popped out of the pages of a fifties fashion magazine. Her bracelet matched her earrings. Her navy-blue pumps matched her navy-blue skirt and polyester, fitted jacket. Her painted face was free advertising for Avon. Her hair (or wig) was piled up to the rafters without one hair daring to peek out. She started scanning me up and down like I was going through airport security.

I deviated from my perfect plan, daring to speak. "Good morning, ma'am" I said with a fake smile. I thought the polite gesture was the right code to let me through this religious checkpoint. Nope. I was wrong.

After her visual inspection, she started into her verbal one. She asked the one question I had feared the most.

"What are you doing here?"

I had rehearsed my answer over and over, but I choked. I wanted to be honest and tell her or anybody who asked, "I'm broken." I wanted to say, "This is my last attempt at finding my misplaced faith," but before I could speak she added, "I don't think God would be too happy with the way you are dressed. Where did you get that outfit, at the Goodwill?"

Trying to think of a witty comeback but finding none, I just said, "Yep." At that time in my life a lot of my clothes had been purchased there. Everything in me wanted to dart out and never go back. This lady is a joke. Who hired her to be the fashion police? Who gave her the keys to the kingdom? I have learned after being in the church for many years now that most churches have these border bullies who keep the church unsoiled by people like me. They are more concerned about how the church looks than how it loves. They come in every color, age, and size. Nobody hires them; they hire themselves. They sadly feel the church would be a much healthier place without sinners.

One man I'd previously seen on the streets tried to convince me to come to his church.

"Why your church?" I asked.

"Because we have no sinners in our church," he proudly stated.

I know you could protest, "Wait, doesn't the Bible say we're all sinners?" and you would be spot-on with your biblical interpretation. If pushed into a corner, these folks will kind of agree with you, explaining your sins are worse than their mistakes. Trust me—you won't win that one.

There were a thousand things I wanted to tell that lady, but they would have gotten me booted out of church and possibly heaven. I smiled, and I in my pink Converses detoured around her, squeezing into the back pew.

I have no clue what the pastor preached on that day. I was so ashamed and depressed. Maybe I should have just played dress-up and wore my funeral suit. I chalked this up to a one-and-done deal with God. Why is it that in the bars people say, "Cookie, I like those pink shoes"? Well, they also say, "You wouldn't catch me dead wearing them." Why is it that the bouncer knows my name and is glad to see me? Why do I feel more love in the bars than I do in the pews?

I was counting down the seconds until the pastor said his final amen. I got up and dashed toward the door. I knew I should have gotten breakfast instead of subjecting myself to this mess. It had turned out just like I had hoped it wouldn't. Oh well, I decided to tell my parents and God I had tried.

As I was inches away from the door and my escape, an elderly woman I had never met before called out my name. "Hi, Dennis," she said with a smile borrowed from an angel.

I stopped and looked at her. Do I know you? She stood there waiting for me to do something. Maybe she got the e-mail, and I'm not in the mood for more looks and laughs. Yet something drew me to her smile.

"How do you know my name?"

"I've watched you play softball."

"Yeah, go on ..."

"Well, I didn't figure you went to church."

I knew it. Now I'd have to go through security to leave the church. She eased my mind with one sentence. "I was praying that one day you would come to our church, and, well, here you are. I'm so excited to see you."

"Really? You mean you prayed for me and actually want me here?"

Her answer was perfect. "Yes, of course. Would you mind if I sit with you next week?"

What I wanted to say was I'm not coming next week, next month, or next year, but what came out of my mouth was, "Yes, I would love that."

"Good. I'll see you next week, Dennis."

Rats. Why did I say yes? I got in my car asking what I had gotten myself into. Now this means I have to come back next week.

But because of this smiling saint I did go to church the following Sunday and the following twenty-eight years of Sundays.

Two old ladies had met me that morning. One wanted me out; the other wanted me in. One didn't like my pink Converses; the other liked the person in them. One thought the church was for saints; the other thought it was for sinners. It's funny how one voice can have the power to hurt or heal. Someone prayed, smiled, and sat with me. I have never forgotten her simple approach to love. I have done my best to duplicate her compassionate kindness with those who feel like the church is against pink Converses and the people who wear them. I'm so glad, looking back, that someone wanted me when I didn't even want myself.

It's funny. Years later the fashion police lady said, "Dennis Cook, I like you."

I said, "I like you too." I teased her for years about our first Sunday security scrutiny. She swore, "Oh, I never would have said that stuff to you," but then she'd add, "but ya know, it wouldn't hurt you to dress up a bit."

She has since died. This may be a bit of the old Dennis leaking out, but I love to imagine her walking though the pearly gates and here comes Jesus, tiptoeing up to her, wearing a short-sleeved shirt, shorts, and pink high-tops. That's a picture I would have loved to see.

I had been pastoring out of town for years and strolled back into my old church and asked a woman I knew how things were going.

"They're going okay."

"I really miss this place," I said.

She leaned in, whispering, "But no one wears pink high-tops anymore." We shared a laugh and went our ways.

I have bored my congregations over the years repeating this story, reminding them that one person has the power to hurt or heal. One person scans and one person smiles. They both have power, one to send sinners back to their messes and others into ministry. We never get a second chance at a first impression.

A few months ago my church gave me a gift during one of our services. To my surprise, it was a brand-new size-ten pair of pink high-top Converse shoes. I laced them up and strutted around the room like I was on a New York runway.

I have no idea if God wears shorts or pink high-tops, but I know for a fact He does love the people who wear them.

15

Jesus and Jack

Some called him a Jesus freak, but to him the label was as tasty as cheese is to a rat. He'd earned it by elbowing Jesus into every tenth word he spoke. He'd collected galaxies of gold stars for faithfully punching into church every Sunday morning and Sunday night. He didn't mind pitching God a few overtime hours by regularly attending Wednesday prayer meetings and local revivals. When he prayed publicly, his prayers lingered on and on, longer than a romance novel. Some jealous newbies wished they'd had his power to shimmy open heaven's doors with such ease. He woke up early each morning to do his daily devotions with the discipline of a soldier and the passion of an evangelist. His closet was stuffed with Christian T-shirts proving he was not ashamed of his God or the gospel. He taught more weekly Bible studies than the pope, if the pope does that type of thing. A worn rosary hung from his bathroom mirror reminded him that prayer changes things.

His living room looked like a knockoff version of the Vatican. He had a museum of framed pictures of Jesus nailed to all four walls. He had thousands of dollars' worth of Christian tapes, CDs, DVDs, magazines, and paperbacks proudly displayed in a dark-brown pressboard bookshelf. Porcelain statues of Jesus and Mary silently collected dust on garage-sale end tables. The white refrigerator was smeared with Christian magnets and cute quotes about miracles and the goodness of God. The kitchen radio was handcuffed to the Christian station, belting out Jesus 24/7 to shoo away unwanted spirits. Baptized in the water and saved by the blood, he had a piece a paper to prove both. His back pocket had a lump due to a miniature Gideon Bible he carried in case of emergencies. His bumper had witty Christian stickers that told others what he was for and against, but mostly against.

If you looked up the word "Christian" in the dictionary, you would see his picture glued alongside Billy Graham's. He was a good man and gave others and God all he had. He freely dispensed grace to people on their way to or from God. Being a former alcoholic, he wept when he thought about all the grace God had used up on his toxic past. Back in his drinking days it was more about guzzling than sipping. If a red solo cup was good, a keg was better. There hadn't been many parties he hadn't crashed. Some were baptized in water and some in whiskey; my friend had been baptized in both.

When telling his story he would exhale with relief, reminding himself and others his past was in the past and God was good. He would always tell me and anyone who would listen what a mess he had been before he'd accepted God's grace. He gave AA and a healing service in the late eighties in Memphis the bulk of the credit for his sobriety and salvation. He felt his deliverance had somehow propelled those nagging imps back to the fiery abyss. His boozeless days had been routinely tallied. "Dennis, I have been clean and sober ten years and seventeen days." He was not afraid to use himself as the punch line for what not to do if it could help straighten out a life. He once said, "Look at me! This is the high cost of low living." This guy was making more than a dent in the world, he was changing it. I can't think of a time when he didn't see more in me than I saw in myself.

Sadly, a few months ago I got a call from his dad. "Dennis, can you go over to my son's house? I think something's wrong. He's not answering his phone." His dad hinted that his boy may have relapsed. For the previous few months he'd been wearing breath mints for cologne. His dad was fearful his boy's old demons were back. I agreed to check on him. When I arrived I was greeted by closed shades and a locked door. I bruised my knuckles knocking, hoping to hear some signs of life. The longer I knocked, the more my mind began to play tricks on me. Hoping for the best and fearing the worst, I jimmied the door open and walked in.

I saw Jesus on the walls and smelled Jack Daniel's in the air. Inspecting around his homemade sanctuary, I called out, "Are you here? Are you alright?" After a few minutes of searching I heard a muffled groan. I tracked down the noise to an upstairs bedroom. When I opened the door, there was the Jesus freak lying in a patch of day-old vomit and snuggling with an empty bottle of Jack Daniel's like it was Raggedy Ann. His face hadn't seen a razor in days, and his eyes hadn't seen the light in years. His hair looked like a bed of wild weeds. His Christian T-shirt was wrinkled and wet from stains of Jack and sweat; my heart ached. So this is what relapse looks like. This is the gloomy conclusion to a man's hidden brawl between his virtues and vices.

"Hey man, what's going on?" I asked.

"Get out of here. I don't need your help!" His words were slurred.

I thought, If somebody doesn't do something soon, this bed could be converted into a casket. All the top-secret late-night rendezvous with Jack had added fifteen years to his face. It looked like his old demons were back after their ten-year, seventeen-day sabbatical. I'd never seen this side of him. I tried to hoist him up to eat and grab a shower, but he just kept saying, "Leave me alone. I don't need you. Leave me alone." His lips, usually overflowing with Jesus, were babbling out four-letter words, telling me and God where we could go. I realized logic and reason were not options, at least right then. I muscled him into a living room chair; he flopped down like a corpse. He sat there with both hands sagging over the armrest, chin drilled into his chest, eyes closed, mouth open. Every few minutes he faded into religious flashbacks, begging God for help and Jack for a drink. He tried to claim Bible verses on healing but couldn't remember the punch lines.

After a few hours of swearing and snoring and gallons of coffee, he finally sobered up enough to recognize who I was. When his eyes opened wide enough to see my face, he started to cry, "Dennis, I'm so embarrassed and ashamed of what I have become! I'm so tired of being shackled to this secret. My math has not been so good. I've been lying about my clean-and-sober tallies." He'd spent the last ten years of his life roaming aimlessly between Jack and Jesus. He loved them both because they made him feel better than he thought he deserved. "I didn't want you, my family, and God to know about my secret," he moaned.

"Well you did a good job hiding it from two out of three of us."

"I felt if I told you the truth you'd walk away like so many others in my life had. Every day I feel like a piece of garbage waking up and wishing I hadn't. You know how I talk about Jesus all the time? Well, it was just a fence I built trying to keep people from knowing who I really was. These pictures and statues are more for luck than love. I hoped God would go soft on a hypocrite like me if I plastered my walls with His pictures."

Without looking at me he mumbled out the truth for the first time in ten years and seventeen days. "Dennis, I lost my faith a long time ago somewhere between Jack and Jesus, and I'm stuck. I know what the Bible says about people like me. I've towed thousands out of the gutter who were stuck, but I can't seem to help myself. It's funny. They used to look at me as a Jesus freak, but when they find out the truth I'll just be a freak. I'm so ashamed of what I've become! What happens when people find out the truth?" He knew the church and how cruel it could be to people like him when they'd fall off the wagon. They got run over by it.

I could already hear the church gossips licking their chops: "Did you hear what happened to Reverend Do-Good? ... Yeah, I heard he's an alcoholic ... No, I heard it was pills ... Yeah, don't say anything, but Sister Snoopy told me the choir director told her he's a crackhead as well. Let's keep that prayer request just between us, okay? ... To think all these years he's been lying to us and God ... Oh well, you know where liars go ... He has nobody to blame but himself. It's his own fault. He made his bed, and now he can lie in it! ... I just don't know why he didn't confide in one of us earlier ... Yes, I was thinking the same thing, but some people are like that, I guess."

"Dennis? There. Now you know the truth. Are you happy? I'm sure God and you are disappointed in me. I let you both down. I would rather you leave me alone. I'll be fine."

I declined his request. "I'm your friend, and I ain't going anywhere. If you think our friendship is based on if you drink Jack, I leave, and stay only if you say Jesus every tenth word, you're wrong." I told my friend, "We are all stuck between Jack and Jesus."

Many of you will say, "Not me, Dennis! I've never seen the bottom of a bottle my whole life!"

Good for you, but you're still stuck. Some are stuck between anger and Jesus, pride and Jesus, lust and Jesus, careers and Jesus, bad marriages and Jesus, death of a child and Jesus, gossip and Jesus. The pews are packed with people stuck between religion and Jesus. We're all stuck, and the people who say they're not stuck seem to be the most stuck. The problem with being stuck is that we take false pride in thinking, Well, at least I'm not as stuck as those people.

I've traveled around the world, and if there's one word that accurately describes its inhabitants, it would be "stuck." People from Africa to Atlanta are stuck. Some are stuck because of their own poor decisions, and others are stuck because of the poor decisions of others. Stuck is the nomadic place somewhere between where you are and where you want to be. Some stay stuck for days and others for decades. Some were born into stuckness, and others will die in it.

Seldom have I met anyone who asked me, "Hey Dennis, can you show me how to get stuck today. Any good advice?" We all, like my friend, find ourselves roaming somewhere between our virtues and vices, between Jack and Jesus.

When we get stuck, we think God wants to hear us fib, "I'm not stuck because I'm a Christian" or "I'm not stuck because I sing in the choir." Can you imagine pulling up next to a car buried in mud to the door handles and asking, "You need a tow?" only to have the driver smile and respond, "Nope!

I'm a Christian, and Christians don't get stuck." That's foolishness; everybody gets stuck and needs a tug or tow every now and then, but we are so scared to admit our stuckness to God, others, and even ourselves.

I believe God loves to hear his children cry out in truth, "God, I'm stuck, and if you don't help me, I'm going down! God, if you don't send me somebody soon I'm going to die in the muck of this mess." We let the shame of our stuckness keep us from asking for tows. But once people admit they are stuck, healing can be right around the corner. We all get stuck, and Jesus is not embarrassed by our stuckness. He drives up, rolls down the window, and asks, "You need a tow?" We have two responses: "Nope, I'm not stuck" or "Yes, and am I ever glad to see You!" I have used both. It had taken being caught in bed with a bottle and then downing a keg of coffee before my friend finally admitted the truth. "Jesus, I'm stuck."

I have been in the church a long time now. I get embarrassed when I keep making the same mistakes over and over again or keep tripping on the same cracks. I feel I should be beyond getting stuck all the time. I feel like people are going to laugh at me when I tell the truth about my stuckness. But most of all I feel God is plain tired of towing me out of the same ditch He has repeatedly warned me to stay away from. So at times, at least for me, it seems easier to just stay stuck and not bother God or others for a tow. My fear is that I'm going to cry out for help and He won't come. I fear He will say, "Nope, I told you to steer clear of that hole a thousand times, so now it's up to you to get yourself unstuck."

My friend taught me that's a lie. He was so desperate and so stuck that all he had was God. No, God didn't show up that night waving a magic wand and presto, my buddy was healed. I've seen God heal some instantly, but for the rest of us it seems like it's one day at a time. It has not been easy for my friend to part ways with his past, but he's trying. He has checked into rehab and is back to counting all over again from the beginning, one day at a time of not being stuck.

Who knows? Maybe the next time it may be you or me sleeping with the bottle, needing a friend more than a sermon, coffee more than criticism. Maybe the next time we see someone stuck between Jack and Jesus we could take some time to talk to them instead of about them.

Some still call him a Jesus freak, but these days he ain't eating the cheese.

16

Praying for Pastors and Playmates

I got one of those calls nobody wants to get. A pastor friend's son had overdosed, and things weren't looking good. When I got to the hospital I saw him leaning against the wall outside the ER. He was understandably devastated, but it was an odd sight because this guy had always been the life of the party. He had one of those charismatic personalities that are magnets to the masses, but that day an unadvertised crisis was quickly erasing his charming personality. His boy's life was in the hands of God and the doctors, but right at that point he had little faith in either.

I cautiously asked him how his son was doing, and he said something I'll never forget. "It's funny. While I'm out saving the whole freaking world, my son's upstairs dying." His eyes were painted red from tears of grief and guilt. He repeatedly questioned how this could have happened. He said what so many who have walked in his shoes before him have said: "I should have been a better parent. I should have seen the signs!" To be a parent with no power to fix the person you love the most is a sobering reality.

We both stood like statues for about a half an hour, pretending to have the right words. He decided it was time to go back to the crammed waiting room as doctors tried to do their magic. As we were heading back in, I saw hospital helicopter touch down several yards from us. I knew if it involved a helicopter it usually meant time was not on a patient's side. I impulsively whispered a short prayer for whoever was inside.

The waiting room looked more like a church service. The small space had been hijacked by a flock of crying parishioners and praying pastors. Many of the same people he had helped navigate through the valley of the shadow of death were now chauffeuring him through. What a beautiful portrait of love on display of what the church should be. For as much bad press as the church gets these days, I thought it got a passing grade that day.

Because there was no room to grab a seat, I slid out into the hall and leaned on the wall. After about an hour of holding up the wall, I saw a petite women slowly meandering down the empty hall toward me. She had bleached-blonde hair with three inches of dark roots tattling on her. She was garbed in a white tank top with a big, bright, pink Playboy bunny stamped on it; her arms were inked with the stories of her life, and her eyes were smudged with dark mascara blotting out her pale cheeks. She was carrying a picture frame in one hand and a wad of crinkled Kleenex in the other. A gold cross hung around her thin neck, possibly more for fashion than faith. Her uncontrollable sobbing was echoing down the hall.

I felt God nudge me to pray with her, but I was a bit scared. I didn't know her; she didn't know me. Plus I was on watch for by buddy's son. I gave myself plenty of good excuses to just keep holding up my wall. I lobbed a silent prayer to God her way and called it good. She did a U-turn and went the other way. I thought, See, God? I was right. It's too late now. As she hiked about thirty feet down the hall, Mr. Guilt started punching me in the belly. I'd felt His jabs before and knew the only way to get Him to stop slugging me was to do the right thing.

Okay, God, if you want me to pray with her, have her turn around and come back my way, amen. I'm not kidding; as soon as I put the period on my prayer she turned around and started walking toward me. I looked the other way; maybe she was meeting someone else? But nope, nothing but me and an empty hall. Now what? What am I supposed to say to her?

I carefully intercepted her path and introduced myself as a pastor. I seldom do that because I get responses like, "Hey I was just thinking about going to church this week, and I'm trying to quit swearing too." But that time I thought it might have given her permission to open up about what she was crying about. I gently eased into the question, "What's wrong?" It's one of those questions you know the answer to, and it won't be, "Ohhh, nothing."

As expected, she gushed out, "My daughter, my daughter. She was running in her seventh-grade gym class and collapsed. The EMS tried doing CPR with no luck. They flew us here in a helicopter a while ago. The doctor just told me she's died, and I don't know what to do. I just keep walking the halls and have no place to go. She can't be dead, right? She's only thirteen. She was just here this morning; I made her strawberry Pop-Tarts for breakfast. Thirteen-year-olds don't die in gym class! What do I do now? I don't know what to do."

She was panting as if she'd just run a 5k. I was obviously one of the first people she had told. She tilted a big school picture of her daughter so I could see it. She proudly said, "Look at her. Isn't she beautiful?" I nodded in sync with words of agreement. She began to recite her daughter's accomplishments and memories as though I were an uncle from out of town. She took the picture and held it to her chest like a child holds a teddy bear. She was twisting her skinny torso left and right as if she were rocking her baby to sleep. She kept repeating "She's gone, she's gone" and crying out "I have nobody! I'm all alone!" If Webster's had a picture next to the word "hopeless," this playmate's picture would be it.

I looked over my shoulder, imagining the "No Vacancy" sign over the waiting room for my pastor friend. There were pastors with their pocket Bibles offering the most appropriate psalms and prayers that could melt and mend any broken heart. Church people had already scheduled meals to be delivered to the pastor's house for a year. Pews of people were letting him know they were there for him, saying, "If there is anything we can do, just let us know." Seldom is there anyone who can do anything to change a father's brokenness and his son's blunder, but it was sure nice to hear it.

She began to talk about the cost of caskets and funerals. Openly she confessed she was not a very spiritual person and had no pastor or church to call home. It was obvious she was at the end of herself. I was not loaded, but I emptied my pockets of cash and coins as an advance on whatever she needed. I offered to do the funeral free of charge. I passed on the church's number and assured her, "If there's anything we can do, let us know."

We both were not sure what to do after that, so we just stood in self-induced silence. I was pleading with God to allow me to offer more than a pocketful of cash. Then I remembered something that had happened a few hours previously. I put the pieces together; this was the gal in the helicopter I had prayed for earlier. I prayed privately God would help that stranger. Now all ninety-seven pounds of that once-stranger was standing in front of me. As I was talking with her I thought, What are the odds of meeting the exact woman in a hospital crammed with more people than some small cities?

I explained, "This sounds crazy, but when you and your daughter flew in on the helicopter, I saw it land and prayed for you. I must admit I never thought I would meet my prayers face-to-face, but I'm glad I did." She was moved by the thought of an outsider praying for them. What I had done silently hours ago God was asking me to do out loud, pray for her, with her.

Although I was a pastor, I had no idea what words to pray to heal grief so raw, so I just let my heart and hurt take the lead. I prayed a very short prayer that God would coach her through the next tricky steps ahead of her. She was overwhelmed that someone would pause long enough to listen to her heartbreaking story. When she left, my prayer did not bring her daughter back to life, but it did breathe a breath of hope into hers. She said, "Thank you for praying for me. It meant a lot."

I went to the crowded waiting room and hung out for the rest of the night, still amazed at what had just happened. God, You go so far out of Your way to show people how much You love them. Not just for the sharp-dressed pastors in suits and shiny cuff links. Not just for the faithful flock that herds in every Sunday. Not just for the saints who paste fish signs on their bumpers. But God, You go out of your way to show Your love to broken, bleach blondes who sport pink Playboy shirts.

Make no mistake about it, the pastor and the playmate both had piles of regrets to sort through from that day on. They both would hear the hiss of demons scolding them that they could have stopped their train wrecks if only they had been better parents. They both had scores of sleepless nights waiting for them that no amount of pills would ease. They both would desperately scream out to a God who seemed more like a spectator than a Savior.

I'm glad God does not look at what we do or what we wear before He helps us. I'm glad God does not look at what we drink or what music we listen to before He helps us. God looks at our hearts, our broken hearts, and He hears our cries whether we are pastors in pinstripes or playmates with pictures.

That day I prayed with a pastor and a playmate who had come from extremely different worlds. One listened to "Amazing Grace," the other to "Free Bird." One took communion to ease the pain, the other tequila. One received piles of prayers that would have made Mother Teresa cry, the other received twenty-one seconds of my rambling to make her cry. One had a twenty-by-twelve-foot crammed waiting room, and the other, well her world had hopelessly shrunk to an eight-and-a-half by eleven walnut picture frame. The good news was God was with them both.

17
Homecoming Dance

It was my senior year of high school and I wanted to go to our homecoming dance. It was not any old homecoming; it would be my very first real dance. It would not be the first time I'd danced; I'd grab my mom's hairbrush for a microphone and do my best Mick Jagger impression in front of our bathroom mirror behind locked doors.

The church I grew up in viewed dancing like alcohol had been viewed in the twenties, sinful and strictly prohibited. It was made clear to us untamed adolescents that going to a dance was one exit shy of Sodom and Gomorrah. Some older church saints, trying to save our souls, whispered, "Dancing is of the devil." We were taught dancing leads to, well you know what … Therefore our church had the rhythm of singing pylons dressed in their Sunday best.

This all created a huge social dilemma for me. Some of my football buddies were enticing me. "Cookie, you have to go to the dance. You're the captain of the team."

It was more peer pressure than I could handle, so I caved in, defiantly boasting, "I'm going to the dance, and I don't care what anyone thinks!" After blurting out this blasphemous blunder, I was afraid. Oh no, what's my dad going to think? What's my church going to think? More than that, what's God going to think? In my juvenile mind that would have for sure punched my one-way ticket to h-e-double-l. But after all, I never wanted to dance with the devil, just a girl, any girl who wouldn't be embarrassed by my maiden trip to the dance floor.

Before I slouched any closer toward Sodom and Gomorrah, I had two huge obstacles, the first being my dad. What complicated this scheme more was that he served as a leader in our church. I rehearsed over and over how I could ask my dad to say no to his convictions and yes to his son. I could have asked my mom, but I knew on matters of dancing with the devil she would defer to a higher power, my dad.

I knew this was going to be a long shot and the answer would be no, so I began to consider some of my religious rebuttals. I tried to remember if the Bible had any loopholes on dancing that would cut through the rolls of red tape our church wrapped around would-be dancers. I was going to tell him he was old-fashioned. I was going to tell him all my Christian friends' (all two of them) parents were letting them go to the dance, but I knew he could pull the old, "If your friends' parents let them jump off a bridge, should I let you?" I was going to make my dad show me a Bible verse that clearly stated, "Dennis Can't Go to a Homecoming Dance." I wasn't really familiar with the Bible, but I was willing to wager that verse was not in there. If that didn't work, my last Hail Mary was to remind him, "I'm almost eighteen, so I can do whatever I want." The only problem with that line of thinking was that my dad was over six feet and a few cheeseburgers past 240 pounds. Plus, I'm not sure if my dad had gotten the memo that spanking a seventeen-year-old wasn't cool.

After mulling over all the possible negative scenarios and my responses, I decided I would simply ask him. On our way to breakfast one Saturday morning I finally got the guts to question heaven's prohibition on dancing. As we pulled into the restaurant, I said, "Dad, I have something to ask you. I know you're going to say no, but I was wondering if you would mind if I go to our homecoming dance." I could almost hear the weeping and gnashing of teeth my pagan request warranted, but before I could get swallowed by the flames below, my dad said yes. I thought the world was coming to an end. I asked him to repeat it, thinking he may have misunderstood me.

It was his surprising yes that led to the second barrier, I couldn't dance. Okay, I could flail around behind locked doors like a fish out of water, but that wouldn't cut it for homecoming. Embarrassingly, I had never danced with a girl in my life; well, maybe with one of my cousins to the chicken dance or the hokeypokey at a wedding, but a guy has only so many left feet to put in and shake all about. The odds were against it, but if by some miracle the DJ played one of those two classics, I was all over it.

So after seventeen long years of waiting, it was finally here, homecoming! As I sifted through my empty closet, I realized I didn't have any dancing clothes. My dad once more stunned me by taking me to Sears to buy a brand-new homecoming outfit. The essential ensemble of the seventies included platform shoes, bell-bottoms, silk shirt, and Old Spice. A gallon. My teen logic reasoned, "If I can't dance good, at least I can try to look and smell good."

But the entire time I was wondering, Why's my Dad doing all this nice stuff for me when I know how he really feels? I didn't want to ask him, feeling he might renege, and back to the brush and bathroom I'd have to go.

After the secular shopping spree we were sitting in the Sears parking lot ready to go home. I looked at my dad, and he was just sitting there looking out the front window. Right then I thought here comes the God guilt speech dropping on me like a bomb. It went something like, "If Jesus were here on earth, do you think He would go to a homecoming dance? Do you think He would give in to peer pressure?" I knew it was too good to be true, but at least I got some new clothes and a keg of cologne out of the deal.

My father turned to the right and interrupted my thoughts with something I will never forget. "I'll always love you, Dennis."

I'm sure I rolled my eyes, robotically responding, "Love you too, Dad."

He knew I hadn't gotten it. He knew I thought they were just words. He'd said them a thousand times before, and for me this was just number one thousand and one. I must admit it seemed like an odd time to tell your son you'd always love him. I'd been bracing myself for a soapbox sermon and got a simple "I love you" instead.

Then he attached one more line to his love. He looked at me and choked out seven more uncomfortable words: "Even if you get a girl pregnant."

Getting a girl pregnant? That involved, well, you know … We didn't talk about stuff like that at home or in church, definitely not before my first homecoming dance! Heck, I was just praying someone would dance with me besides the devil.

He continued, "I just wanted you to know there's nothing you could possibly do that I wouldn't love you."

My mind race back and forth to the things I had done and the things I wanted to do, and not all would be sanctioned by the church, him, or God. And then it hit me; my dad in his own timid way was saying there were no limits to his love. "There is nothing you could do that would make me love you more or less." At that moment my world stopped; I had heard my dad say he loved me countless times, but this time it was different. Up to that point I'd thought he'd loved me more if I had made the game-winning shot, if I had scored a touchdown or had gotten Cs on my report card. (We had kind of low academic standards for my life back then). I don't think any bad thing I would have told him at that moment could have gotten him to recant his statement of love. He was saying what every young boy wants to hear from his dad: "I love you, son."

I'm many birthday cakes past seventeen now. I'm married and have two teenage daughters. Sometimes, when life gets tough, I drive back to that Sears parking lot and sit there. I reminisce about those awkward yet simple words my dad shared that day. There are times I would trade a thousand days for that one, days when I blow it with my wife and kids … days when my past catches up with my present … days when all I see is all I'm not … days I'm more lost than found. Those days I wish I could go back to that clumsy moment in a Sears parking lot a long time ago.

I now know it was a moment a father was letting go of his son to be a man. It was also a moment a son wanted to hold on to his father and still be a boy. He knew I was stuck in that teenage wasteland somewhere between puberty and pimples. It was the day I learned my dad loved me more than he loved the rules of the church. It was the day I learned what unconditional love really looked like, my dad.

In case you're interested, my first homecoming dance was a dud. I sat on a metal chair most of the night as a spectator, watching others twist and shout. I finally got enough nerve to ask a girl to dance, and out of pity she said yes. All that drama for one slow dance, and you could have placed the Grand Canyon between us.

I never danced with the Devil that night … I never got a girl pregnant that night … I never got a kiss, but I did get a handshake. Not quite the ending I had anticipated, so I figured it was back to the brush and bathroom for me.

I am now a parent, and I drag my daughters to church each Sunday. They ask me to go to dances all the time without fear of plunging into the flaming abyss. They lure me into taking them shopping for homecoming dresses that cost more than the car I'd driven to that homecoming. Now I'm telling my girls what my dad told me many years ago in that Sears parking lot, "I love you, and there's nothing you can do about it."

They look at me and roll their eyes and robotically respond, "Love you too, Dad."

18

Twelve Empty Chairs

Iremember the night my wife and I prayed for a baby. It was not, as it is for so many, that we could not have one, for this would be our second. Our first child had been born without any complications and was beautiful. All we were doing was asking God to stamp His blessing on our prayers and pregnancy. I wasn't sure if this was a real prayer or just a religious formality; either way, after our amen, we felt it truly was God's will for us to have another child.

It didn't take long before my wife gave me the news. "Dennis, I'm pregnant."

I'm sure I did some stupid, happy dance to celebrate the stork flying our way. We immediately began the process of digging through libraries of baby name books. The next decision was what color to splash on the walls, pink or blue. We leaked the good news out, and within days people from our church started dropping off his-and-her clothes at our doorstep. Life was good in the Cook family.

But one late night that all changed. It was about three in the morning when I was awakened by a piercing screech coming from behind the bathroom door. I thought it was a dream, but the volume increased.

"Oh God, Oh God, help me, please help me! Den, come help me!"

I leaped out of bed and opened the bathroom door and saw my wife lying on the floor in the fetal position. I had never heard her scream that loud before. I am not a person who handles suffering well, especially when it involves my family.

I panicked, not knowing what to do. She told me to call a woman from our church who was a nurse. I quickly dialed the number, waking her up, gasping, "Please tell us what to do! Heidi's lying on the floor screaming."

"Dennis, get her to the hospital immediately. I'm sorry to tell you, but I think Heidi could be losing the baby."

I was so shocked to actually hear those words slip out of her mouth. I wanted to say, "How do you know? You're no doctor!" but it was no time to squabble over her phone diagnosis. I picked up my wife and carried her to our car. I think I drove 200 miles an hour and ran every stop sign without remorse. I flew into the hospital parking lot in our small town, flung the door open, and carried my wife to the ER entrance. I knocked on the door, but nothing. I kept knocking, but no one was coming to our rescue. I started to kick the door and scream for help. After putting a dozen size ten and a half dents in the door, someone finally opened it. I was ticked off. How in the heck can the ER be locked?

A woman asked, "May I help you?"

"Ah, yes, you can help my wife here draped in my arms." After several questions about insurance and social security numbers they wheeled her in to the emergency room and asked me to wait outside.

After hours behind closed doors a doctor came out and confirmed the worst. "Mr. Cook, I'm so sorry, but you've lost the baby, and your wife had a lot of internal bleeding. We have a few things to do to stabilize her, and then you can see her. Do you have any questions?"

I didn't know what to ask or say. I think I said thank you as if he had just served me ice cream or something.

I sat in the empty waiting room, feeling numb. What was crazy was that I'd sat in the same chairs giving advice to several grieving families who had been forced to choke down the same dreadful news, but I had nothing to give myself. I tried to recall some of the wisdom I had passed their way, but all I could do was think that our baby was dead and try to figure out whose fault it was.

Maybe I should have woken up faster. Maybe if I was stronger I could have gotten her to the car quicker. Maybe if I'd driven 300 miles an hour instead of 200. And why was that dumb door locked? Why should a person have to a kick down a door to get help? What if they had skipped all that "What's your name and social security number, and do you have insurance?" jazz and had just taken her into surgery. Couldn't they have figured all that out after they'd saved our baby?

I felt so alone surrounded by twelve empty chairs, three coffee tables, one lamp, and stacks of outdated gossip and good-parenting magazines. The night nurses were going home and the day nurses were beginning their shifts. One nurse bounced in, with no clue as to why I had been sitting there, saying, "Good morning, sir, what a great morning! Can I get you a cup of coffee? Decaf or regular?"

Decaf or regular? We've just lost our baby and you're asking me about coffee? I had no idea how to respond, so I didn't. I wasn't blaming her for doing her job; I felt I was blaming God for not doing His.

The questions were flowing out of my heart like hot lava, setting fire to every dream we had had for our baby. The thing that had me all worked up is that we had prayed. We had told God, Hey, if you want us to have a baby, fine, and if you don't want us to, that's fine. But then I was thinking I swear I thought you gave us the green light to have this baby. Maybe this is some heavenly gag you play on Christians just to see if they'll still blow you kisses when you rip life out of their hands, but if it is, I'm not laughing, and neither is my wife, who would have gladly given up her life to save that baby.

I know this because she had told me, "Dennis, if it's me or the baby, save the baby. I've prayed over this, and it's okay." I couldn't confirm or deny her request because either way I'd lose; I just nodded my head in silence, indicating, I heard ya, Heidi.

Why would a loving God wave you through a green light only to allow a semi loaded with nothing but grief, guilt, and answerless questions take you and your dreams out?

If You were going to give us good news only to renege a few months later, what's the point? It seems to me You should have said no when we asked. Yes, I know we would have whined, kicked, and screamed over Your veto to our request, but this? This seems cruel!

It was just me and twelve empty chairs in a waiting room, wondering what I was going to say to my wife. I was a pastor after all, and I felt I had to be strong for her. I didn't want to start crying and make it worse. I made a vow on the spot to lock up my tears for another day, a day when it was just me alone somewhere, anywhere, but not in that waiting room.

My thoughts were interrupted by a much more compassionate nurse who knew why I was there, who invited me back to see my wife. I asked God, who I wasn't too thrilled with, to help me help her. I walked into the room, saw her face, and knew she was thinking the same thing I was. What went wrong? Her face was soaking wet from crying. I nestled up as close as I could to her bed, grabbed her hand, and kept trying to speak, but nothing would come out. I wanted so badly to say something to ease the damage that this semi had caused, but nothing came out. I had given barren and broken women gobs of advice, but for my own wife I had nothing. I did not pretend. I just sat thinking about my wife's now empty womb and broken heart.

After a few hours of silent love the doctors asked me to leave so my wife could get some rest. Funny how I'm running night and day all over the state to make sure everybody has somebody to sit and cry with, and yet I'm sharing one of the most miserable nights of my life with twelve empty chairs.

Exhausted, I collapsed into the open arms of one of the twelve. I closed my eyes, pretending it was all just a bad dream, that I would wake up and things would be back to good again, back to baby names and wall colors.

Then I heard a familiar voice. "Hey Dennis, what are you doing here?" Carl, who went to my church, was a guy I'd been hammering over the head for the previous two months to go to the doctor's. He had some heart problems but was too stubborn to get it checked out.

He repeatedly told me, "I ain't going to the hospital, and you can't make me!"

So I was shocked to see him there.

"Who are you here visiting this early in the morning?"

I told him I'm not here for someone else. This was not the guy who would have won the "Most Spiritual Man" award in our church or any church. Carl and God didn't see eye-to-eye on very many things. He had way more questions than answers. I'd heard Carl say some things to and about God that caused me to dive away in fear of lighting. Carl was a broken man who had chalked up more losses than victories in life. He had just gone through a divorce and was rarely in a good mood because of it; when he'd lost his wife he'd lost his life.

God, this is the only guy in the Western hemisphere who is probably madder at You than I am right now, so can you please send me someone more like Billy Graham or Mother Teresa to help heal this gash?

After I gave him the details as to what had happened, he was moved to tears. Is Carl crying? He never cries!

He kept repeating, "I am so sorry for you and Heidi." He called dibs on one of the twelve chairs for the entire day. He never gave me one verse or patronizing sermonette; he just filled an empty chair. Every few minutes I would look over, and he would be crying, pretending he wasn't. He would ask me over and over if he could get me anything.

I just kept thinking *What I want you can't give me.*

"Why are you here, Carl?"

"Don't you know? I'm here because of you."

"What're you talking about?"

"You kept begging me to go to the hospital, and I woke up today and thought, 'Dennis is right,' and here I am."

"Oh yeah? Then how come you're not getting checked out?"

"I cancelled my appointment when I saw you sitting here; I can get checked out another day. It's kind of spooky—here you've been bugging me to go to the doctor's, and today is the day I picked, the day you need me. It's always me needing you, but today you need me. Even I know that's God."

Still ticked off, I tried baiting Carl into some good ol' God bashing with me. He usually swallowed the bait with a smile. Anything to do with God not coming through or being fair, he was always all in. This guy had a list as long as the Ohio Turnpike of things God had not come through on. It was always me beating into his noggin how good God was. But that particular day he was having nothing to do with being baited or bashing. That day Carl was so full of the love of God I hardly recognized him. I'd never seen that side of him, and I was sure he'd never seen this side of me.

I peeked over my shoulder his way and thought, I'm so glad God sent me Carl and not Graham. God sent me someone who knows what brokenness is. He sent me someone familiar with losing someone he loved. He sent me someone who's not scared of my suffering and silence.

Carl occupied one of the twelve chairs all day without saying much of anything, yet I felt I was sitting next to God Himself.

I still don't know why God allows what He allows. Why does He give a baby to one mom who tosses the absolute gift into a dumpster five minutes after delivery and give another begging lady putting dents in heaven's door for twenty-three years no answer at all? God doesn't consult with me on His decisions on matters of life and death, on who gets a baby and who gets twelve empty chairs, because if He did I wouldn't be writing this story right now.

When my wife and I went back to our church, I was overwhelmed by how many of the ladies told us they too had lost babies. I had been pastoring these people for years and had had no idea. One woman was so hurt for us that she told her story of loss, the first time she had ever told her story to anyone. I thought, Wow, there are so many people carrying stories of loss all around us.

It's been over fifteen years since our child died. People have moved on with their lives. No one ever asks about it anymore. I guess I understand, but it would be nice to hear someone say, "We're thinking of you. You're not forgotten." Yet I too can get so busy doing Jesus stuff I forget people's past hurts while trying to offer them future hope.

I sat in that waiting room all those years ago promising myself I would cry another day, but that day never came. I guess I was so mad at God. I had been kicking down heaven's door and nobody had come to our rescue. I felt we got cheated on our prayers back then. I felt the best thing was to ignore it and move on. I'll see our baby in heaven someday.

I have kept my tears under lock and key all these years, but today I'm sitting in a crowded McDonald's writing this story, and I can't stop crying. Fifteen years of hidden hurt, brokenness, disappointment, and a runaway semi are dripping all over my laptop.

It's crazy, but it feels good to cry. I can't believe I have buried my emotions all these years thinking I was strong when I've just been mad. I feel like I blew it by trying to be strong for my wife then and now. How can you lose a baby and never talk about it with each other? I'm sure my wife wanted to talk, but I was the one who kept life moving on to not get stuck in the past. I don't know … maybe it would have been better for both us if I had walked into her hospital room that night and cried my eyes out. By trying to help her I think I hurt her. I have made her carry the bulk of our pain by burying mine; maybe I should have spent less time bashing God and more time talking with my wife.

You and I know marriages that could not survive the loss of a child. They start out being there for each other, but after time and pain take their toll, they slowly drift their separate ways. The hurt gets so bad and buried so deep they feel no one understands them. They always talk to each other but seldom say anything. When they lie in bed at night they both stare at the ceiling, wondering what might have been. They are living every day of their lives stuck in one, the day they lost their child. They no longer see what they have, only what they have lost. The funeral has caused an awkward amnesia between them, forgetting their vows for better or worse. Their relationship has been demoted from marriage to simply roommates who share the bills and a bed.

Then one day he comes home from the gym and his wife has packed up twenty-nine years of marriage in a suitcase and gives him back his ring and last name. After a too many years of suffering alone she feels it would be better if they both went their separate ways and tried to start life over with someone else, someone more fun.

I have buried this emotion long enough. If I don't do something soon, it will bury me. When we lost our baby it was early in the pregnancy. We didn't have a funeral, and we didn't know the right thing to do back then. We told a few people and moved on. At least I did.

So today I'm sitting in a McDonald's, surrounded by fifty strangers and a porcelain statue of Ronald McDonald, having a funeral for our child we lost fifteen years ago. I'm crying, praying, and thanking God not for our loss but for His walking us through it. I'm still clueless as to what went down that crazy night fifteen years ago, but today I'm not mad at God. I'm sure God and I will have plenty more lovers' spats in the future, but not today. I'm so glad God does not get mad at me when I get mad at Him. I'm so glad

God does not dump us when we dump Him. I'm so glad He is big enough to handle my doubt and fears without holding a grudge.

When I decided to write this story my aim was to help someone else being swallowed up by twelve empty chairs. To someone who can't climb out of the past no matter how hard they try. To someone who is not on speaking terms with God at the moment. To someone who feels their heart is as empty as the dusty crib still sitting in pink or blue room. But I had no idea writing this story would be the first step toward healing something I didn't think was broken, my heart.

19

Recess

Have you ever had days you wish you could take a recess from being a Christian? Sadly, I do. There are days I wish I didn't have to live out my faith in a fishbowl. I want to rip off my Christian fish, if I had one, from my bumper, letting my inner NASCAR out to zoom over the speed limit without getting ticketed by the police or God. I want to leave my Jesus T-shirts neatly tucked in the top drawer. I feel like copping the fifth on all questions concerning why bad things happen to good people. It's not that I don't love people or God or want to resign; I just want what all third graders get every day: recess.

I had one of those days, okay, months, at the first church I pastored. I didn't have a clue what I was doing there. I felt undereducated and overwhelmed. It seemed like the harder I worked at trying to fix people the more they broke. All I ever wanted to do was help people, but then I was the one who needed help. The stress of so many broken lives had kicked all my joy to the curb.

So I decided, after a few years of foolishly working through my vacations, to kidnap my family and head to Florida. Michigan springs have been known to play hide and seek until July. The stress and snow had enticed me to slide down I-75 South until we bottomed out on white sand.

I'll tell you how stressed out I was. As my family and I were leaving for our spring fling with our car packed to the tippy-top, I robotically drove into the church parking lot to do my religious duties for the day as I did every day. I got out of our car and marched straight into my church office as I did every day. I went in, sat behind my computer, punching in for Jesus. I looked out the window and realized I had made a minor mistake. My family was still in the car that I had left running, thinking I had finally, truly lost my mind. I realized my stressful gaffe and sheepishly slid back into the car, hoping they wouldn't notice or laugh. They did both for the next 200 miles.

With every mile of Michigan I left in the rearview mirror, I daydreamed about the beach and doing nothing but emptying a few jugs of Coppertone. I selfishly wanted to retreat to an oasis where I would not be known as Pastor Dennis. I dreamed of a few days of no counseling, no preaching, no studying, no weddings, no funerals, and no helping God fix the world. I wanted one week being my wife's husband and my daughters' dad. I wanted one week with my family to do absolutely nothing all day long and wake up the next day and do it all over again.

One afternoon, late in our shrinking week, Mackenzie, our six-year-old, and I journeyed to the grocery store. We walked out with our hands full of bags bulging with picnic goodies.

As we drove out of the parking lot we hit a red light. Off to my right was a scruffy man holding a cardboard sign. I didn't have to look at the sign to know what it said. I reminded myself, You're on vacation … You're on vacation … Dennis, you can't save the whole world. I was also reminding God, in case He had forgotten, that I was on vacation and I'd punch back in when I saw Florida in my rearview mirror. I offered excuse after excuse to guarantee that those picnic snacks in the bag ended up in my stomach.

I turned my head and prayed not for the man but rather that the red would turn green so we could speed off. Seconds before my prayer was answered, Mackenzie spoke.

"Dad, what does that man's sign say?"

"Ahh, what man, honey?"

"The one standing right in front of you."

Justifying my intentional blindness, "Honey, daddy gives money all year long to many people. We sponsor a child overseas, and today we'll let someone else be blessed to help him." It's a pretty sad day when you're giving your six-year-old daughter your résumé of all your good deeds for the year. But she was buying none of what I was selling.

She repeated her question. "Daddy, what does his sign say?"

I sheepishly interpreted his cardboard prayer, mumbling, "He needs food, Mackenzie."

Her face lit up like she'd just personally solved global poverty. She looked at me. "Hey, Dad, we have food. Can we give him ours?"

"Oh yeah, I guess we can."

So I pulled over, and we did. It was so simple for her kindergarten faith: we have food, he needs food, one plus one equals two, give him food.

I love the elementary lesson Mackenzie taught me that family vacation: poverty gets no recess, no vacations, no days off. I was much more proud of her than I was of me.

I still have days when the stress of life can completely strangle the joy out of my job. I still have days I covet the beach more than the Bible, lots of those. I still have days when it seems easier to resign than refuel. And yes, I'll admit, I still have way too many days I wish for a recess from being a Christian. But what my daughter taught me when she was six I'm still working on at fifty: it's alright to take a recess from your job, but never from your faith. I know. I tried it.

20

42" Levee

Just saying the word "Katrina" can scrape off an old scab that just doesn't heal. To some it means more than others. If you're from the North, as I am, it's flashbacks of devastating pictures via satellite into our living rooms 24/7. If you're from the Midwest, your community's population may have spiked a bit by the displaced. But if you're from New Orleans the word steals your breath away.

I was able to watch the whole disaster using my forty-two-inch TV as a levee to protect me from the sights and sounds of the storm. From the comfort of my leather couch I could watch desperate people on roofs. I could watch people stealing Hostess cherry pies from convenient stores while I was fixing my family's dinner. When it all got too much I could always exit their world with a push of a button from mine.

I went to New Orleans on a mission trip almost two years after Hurricane Katrina with about a dozen folks from Michigan. After getting there I realized not a lot had changed. People were still just as ruined as the buildings that surrounded them. The entire trip I kept thinking the devastation was so much larger than my large-screen TV could display. We had a fantastic week of serving strangers and making friends.

On one of our last nights in New Orleans we drove a trailer stocked with sorted clothes, bags of food to place called Tent City, a downtown park shouting distance from the mayor's office. This huge chunk of land was full of families still calling six-by-eight tents home. It was hard to watch all the kids forced to live like Boy and Girl Scouts on permanent campout.

The temperature was just cool enough that you could see your breath. By the time we opened the trailer doors a crowd had already lined up for coats, blankets, socks, and whatever would keep them and their children warm. They were able to walk in the back of the trailer and out the front. My station was near the front of the trailer, finding the right size shirts and pants.

What caught me off-guard was how nice all the people were. You would think living in a tent for so long would make folks a little cranky, a lot cranky, but the people we met were so grateful for shirts and pants even two sizes too big. They hid their scars well. As people would come through the end of line I would ask them if they wanted prayer. Not one person turned a prayer away. One man, after I prayed for him and his family, placed his hand on my shoulder and asked, "What's your name?"

"Dennis."

"Can I pray with you, Dennis?"

When he asked me what to pray for, I had nothing. Don't get me wrong—I had plenty of things I was praying for in Michigan, but thousands of miles South I had somehow forgotten them.

He closed his eyes and began to pray. "Ah God, I pray for Dennis, I pray you will bless him and his family—You do have a family, right?"

"Yes I do."

"God, I pray you will just bless him real good for coming down and helping us, amen."

I thanked him with a bear hug that I'm sure cracked a few ribs.

I learned part of doing this type of outreach was just taking time for people to tell you their sides of the story. As we were running out of stuff, one man came up and sparked some small talk. Where we were from? Why we were there? Did we have families?

I asked the Katrina question, which always got me a thousand different answers that all flowed into one word, "hurt." In precise detail he began to replay a day he would always remember but would always try to forget. He began with where he had been when the storm hit and why he hadn't left the city. He asked, "Where can you go if you have no place to go?" For a few minutes he imitated a weatherman retelling a two-year-old forecast. Then it got personal. He looked at me and asked, "Do know what it's like?"

I was not sure where his line of questioning was headed, so I stayed silent.

The volume of his voice went up. "Do you know what it's like to have water rushing into your house?" Turning it up louder, he asked, "Do you know what it's like to lose all your possessions? To see all the things you worked your whole life for floating down your driveway?"

The conversation moved from dialogue to monologue, and the volume went up to full blast with anger and rage. "Do you know what it's like to watch your wife and children hopelessly float down the street?" He paused, trying to catch his breath. Though his body lived in a tent, his mind lived in a storm. He lamented. "I tried. I really did try to save them. One's floating this way and the other's floating that way—what do you do?" His head slumped over as he whispered to anyone close enough to hear or care, "Do you know what it's like?"

I mentally grilled myself. Why did I ask a question I knew would pull off his scab? I should have just kept my mouth shut and passed out clothes. I had no comeback or clever counsel. Years ago I'd heard this type of story over and over again coming from my big TV, but then, hearing it without a remote, was a lot tougher. I felt it was an awful way to end the day and our week in New Orleans. Just when I thought he would hobble off in defeat to his tent, he lifted his head. Here it comes. He's going to snap. I took a few steps back and prepared for the worst.

Then two of the most beautiful words bravely came out of his mouth. "But God."

"What?" I asked, thinking I had missed something.

He said, "But God. If not for God I would have no tent to sleep in; if not for God, I would have starved to death; if not for God and Burger King, I would have no place to bathe; if not for God, I would have lost my mind a long time ago. The only peace I have is knowing my wife and kids are safe and sound with Him. It may not look like it when you look at me or where I live, but man, I'm blessed."

Did he just say "blessed"? If he did, I need to look up that word in the dictionary again! I've heard many people with new cars, new clothes, new jobs, and new relationships say they were blessed, but this guy has lost it all but a six-by-eight tent. This guy lives off strangers showing up serving soup and sandwiches. This guy uses the Burger King bathroom for a Laundromat, shower, and place to change, and he's saying he's blessed! I've never heard people who have lost it all say they were blessed simply because they still had God.

I've bragged to God and others for years that I was blessed, but usually it was because I had all the stuff this guy had lost. I was blessed because I had a nice car, nice house, nice children, and a family who loved me, and I lived in America. I'd never had to go without a meal or wash in a Burger King bathroom. I'd never had to live in a tent. (Well, my wife and I did try the camping thing for a weekend, but that almost caused a divorce.) Through this New Orleans saint I saw a brand-new definition of "blessed." He felt he was blessed not for what he had but rather for who had him.

I stood there with no 42" levee to protect me. No remote to turn the station. No couch to retreat to. I wanted to leave him with some grand piece of wisdom as a parting gift, but it seemed he was the teacher and I was the student.

He said, "Thanks for asking how I'm doing. Not a lot of people around here ask that question anymore because we all know the answer."

We hugged each other and said, "See ya later," both knowing the odds were against it.

21
Parking-Lot Confessions

Our church was trying to raise some money to send our kids to camp by collecting empty cans. It was a great success, but a few days later I saw a leftover bag of empties at the church that hadn't made it to the store. I grabbed a friend from the church and said, "Let's drive around and look for someone who's searching for empties."

We drove out of the church parking lot, got a few miles down the road, and there he was, a man riding a rickety old bike from 1972 in the Big Lots parking lot with a white trash bag slung over his shoulder, combing the ditch near the store, looking for empties. We pulled up next to him and asked him his name. He was a drop slow to give out such personal information to a couple of strangers, but he eventually said "Ken" and kept on cycling.

I said, "Ken, just wondering if you wanted to take this bag of cans off our hands."

"What's the catch?"

"There's no catch, just a bagful of empties. Would you like the cans?"

Ignoring the question, he went into a long-winded explanation as to why he had been riding his bike and picking up cans. "I was in a car accident; my car was totaled trying to swerve around a cat. Can you believe it, trying to miss a crazy cat?" He gave us an animated play-by-play of the feline mishap. He wanted us to know it was the cat's fault, not his, that his car had been totaled.

When he finally came up for air, I casually said, "We've just opened a new church down the road, and you're invited." I eased his mind that there were no dress codes or membership dues; he just had to show up. I told him I was the pastor, and he could be my personal guest.

Before I could say another word, he bellowed out, "I'm a sinner."

I glanced at my friend. Did he just say what I thought he said? It's not that he stuttered; it's simply that you usually don't hear those words out loud let alone in public. I responded, "So am I."

He said in a guarded yet confident voice, "But you know what? God forgives sinners. Isn't that good news?"

"Yes, that's great news for the both of us." Wow! We went from talking about cans and cats to Christ in sixty seconds flat! Just think; when was the last time you heard someone unsolicited declare "I'm a sinner" publicly? I mean, if you bully people into a corner with guilt and lay a King James whuppin' on them, maybe, just maybe, you can force a confession out of them. I have a hard time saying I'm a sinner in my private prayers with no one around, and I'm a pastor, but this guy just hollered it out in a public parking lot to a couple of strangers.

After his parking-lot confession he said, "Yes, I'll take the cans but not sure of the church thing."

"Okay, Ken, nice meeting you." I said.

He pedaled off, balancing his bike with two bulging bags of cans to his right and left.

I got back in my truck completely confused by this stranger's confession, not what he had said but why he had said it. What prods a man to tell complete strangers he's a sinner? Who told him he was a sinner? How does he know God forgives? Why had this guy been so anxious to reveal what so many of us Christians try to conceal? Then I thought about how in church we preach hellfire and brimstone sermons, sing three hymns and three choruses, and close with sixty-five verses of "Just As I Am," repeating after each one, "This is the last time" all to persuade people to a place of honesty to simply say, "God, I'm a sinner and I need your help and forgiveness." Yet this guy, with no sermon,songs or sanctuary, with just a bike and a bag of empties, had confessed who he was and who God is.

His words were so simple and satisfying. He didn't seem like he was trying to impress me or God; he was just telling it like it was. He didn't beat himself up over his sin, and he didn't ignore it; he did what the Book says to do: "If we confess our sin, God is faithful to forgive." I, on the other hand, either beat myself up till I draw blood or justify it by blaming others for my transgressions. Seldom do I say, "God I'm a sinner, forgive me," and move on with my day; that seems too simple.

The more I pondered Ken's parking-lot confession, I thought. Why not 'fess up? Why not just say I'm a sinner? Jesus says he's a friend of sinners.

Jesus forgives sinners. Jesus died for sinners. The Bible says we all have sinned and have fallen short of what God wants. Paul, who penned most of the New Testament, says about himself, "I'm the least of the apostles, I'm least of all the saints, and I'm a chief sinner." Not exactly the hallowed words you expect to come from Paul's holy lips. Saint Paul and Saint Ken both knew what many believers forget: confession brings a freedom to be real with God and others.

I thought if Ken could confess he was a sinner in a parking lot, it probably wouldn't hurt me to say it in my private prayers. I have spent a lot of loot on fancy-dancy leadership conferences, but this life lesson cost me just fifteen minutes and some empties. What was so cool about Ken was that he had found in a parking lot what we often miss in church: God loves sinners.

Oh yeah, one more thing. He also forgives them.

22

Cleanup on Aisle Seven

Cancer has a way of bringing even the strongest to their knees and leaving them begging for mercy. Cancer has no conscience as to whose life it will pummel. It will pounce on a five-year-old as easily as on a seventy-five-year-old, and when the fight is over, it stands up and defies anyone to beat it. Many have tried, but only a few have won.

My mom was one of those chosen few who had drawn the short straw. She was the most fun person to be around and lived life to the fullest. She loved us kids more than she loved herself. When she found out she had cancer, she didn't want to tell us kids due to the pain it would inflict on us. When she did leak it out, it was as if she were telling us she had a cold. "Oh, just wanted you to know I have cancer, but don't worry; a little chemo here and there and I should be good as new soon." As is the case with so many, soon never came.

Two stolen breasts later, it was not going away. Her hair had fallen out, so she was embarrassed to go out in public. She'd worn a wig in the early seventies because she wanted to; after cancer, because she had to. She would lock herself in the bathroom, staring into the mirror, viewing all cancer had stolen with no intention of ever giving it back. You could hear her cry leaking out under the door.

Sometimes she would sit in some ugly, green chair she'd found at a garage sale for days at a time, crying.

"What's wrong, mom?"

"Oh, nothing, this darn chemo's just hurting a bit." Then she would ask me if I wanted to watch "Wheel of Fortune" and "Jeopardy" with her. She said "Wheel of Fortune" made her feel smart and "Jeopardy" made her feel dumb.

I laughed, "Mom, that's the way everybody feels."

One night I decided to call dibs on my old bed, still in the same place I'd left it when I'd turned eighteen and moved out and on with life. Part of me was wishing I could rewind the clock to when I was a boy, when this small bed fit my big feet. I wished I could go back to when my mom was just my mom minus cancer and chemo. After an hour or so of wishing wishes that would never come true I feel asleep.

I woke to a strange sound about 4 a.m.; I got up to see what it was. I took one step out of my bedroom and into the living room and saw my mom curled up in her ugly, green chair with both hands over her mouth, trying to cry quietly.

"Mom, what are you doing?"

"Den, I'm so sorry if I woke you. I tried not to wake you up."

"Mom, who cares? Why are you crying?"

"Oh this chemo thing …"

"No, mom, why are you crying?"

"I don't want to tell you."

"Mom, please tell me why you're crying."

Suddenly she lost it. I'd never seen her cry so uncontrollably. I'm sure she had, but she had always done her best to keep this type of anguish behind closed bathroom doors to protect us kids. I was wishing I hadn't asked.

"I wish I could die, just die. I don't want to fight anymore. I feel such a burden on all you kids. I think you all would be better off without me. You could sell the house and help pay for some of my overdue doctor bills. I don't want you kids to have to pay for my debt of my disease."

My mom is a Christian and one of the godliest women I know. She gave being a Christian a good name. She said, "I watched a special on TV last night. It was about that Jack Kevorkian guy or however you say his last name. They were showing how he helped suffering people … die. Den, I never believed in that kind of stuff before, but now …"

She never finished her sentence. I asked no more questions. Cancer was stretching her and her faith so thin I was waiting to hear them both snap with one more punch.

At the time she was still working a few days a week at a retail store to keep from going crazy with all the cancer stuff. It was so weird to look at my once-strong, thick-boned mom so thin. Her T-shirt clung vertically to her flat chest. She had a few stray, grey hairs poking from her scalp just to tease her. She would look in the mirror and say, "Den, I think my hair's coming back. Maybe God will heal me."

I just nodded and said, "That's what we're praying for, Mom."

Just when you think things can't get any worse they do; Mom called me from work bawling one day.

"Den, I'm so embarrassed!"

"What happened?"

"I don't know if I should tell you I'm so ashamed. Can you just stop by?"

When I got to her house I asked again, "What happened?" I thought the chemo was making her sick again.

She said, "I was stocking shelves like I always do, and uh, uh ..."

"What, Mom?"

"Den, I'm so embarrassed. My bowels let loose, and I went to the bathroom in my pants, and the mess ran down my legs and onto the floor. It stunk so badly, and I was so mortified I just stood there in my mess and cried. I wanted to run and hide, I wanted to die. How could God let something like this happen to me, especially in public? Then someone trying to help broadcast over the loudspeaker, 'Cleanup on aisle seven.' Den, I was never so humiliated!"

Caring for others, she lamented the poor stock boy who had to clean up her mess. Imagine the grace of this minimum-wage kid who had gotten down on all fours and cleaned up my mom's mess, saying, "That's okay, Mrs. Cook, I got this." I'd been a stock boy back in the day, and I'm not sure if those would have been my exact words.

So my mom was feeling not only a burden at home but also at work. I tried to say something to make it all better; it was only what she had done for me my whole life. No matter how big my messes were, she always seemed to have just the right words to make them all better. Our roles had reversed; I was the parent and she was the kid, and neither of us could do anything about it.

She was always so positive, thinking the best of people and circumstances. She had bravely taken this fight into extra rounds, but after the day's "aisle seven" embarrassment, I could see her arms slowly dropping to her side. I could see her one punch away from throwing in the towel.

Me, pretending to be full of faith, snatched the white towel from her and said, "We're going to fight this thing and won't give up," but she didn't respond to my pep talk and phony, faith-healer sermon.

A few months later she'd finally had enough. She put her hands down in submission, and cancer drew back and delivered one more haymaker that put her in a coma. She was in a hospital room, her skin almost the same color as that ugly, green chair she used to befriend; she couldn't open her eyes or talk; she could just mumble.

I'd coached her for years to fight, fight, fight and don't give up because you can beat this monster. With God all things are possible, but that day I stared at her frail frame renting half a single hospital bed. She was lying there, exhausted and panting for her next breath.

I wanted to scream into her coma, "Mom, stay down, stay down, it's not worth the fight anymore, quit. It's okay, it's okay, it's time. We kids will be okay," but I loved my mom so much that I protected my heart instead of hers and cheered for her to get up and fight again.

You could hear her choke and cough, moving her mouth but saying nothing. It was like she was trying to drag herself up the ropes to fight another round to not let us kids down. I was standing by her bed with the white towel clenched in my hands, not having the courage to toss it in. At one time, minutes, hours, even days with my mom meant nothing because I always knew I would get more. I was feeling so selfish because I was then begging God for a few more seconds.

I leaned down and grabbed her hand, saying "I love you, Mom" over and over. It was all that would come out. It was funny—the many things I wanted to tell her were all reduced to four words. Then, without my consent, God stole the towel out of my hands and tossed it into the ring. Just like that it was over. No more chemo, no more gasping for air, no more fighting, no more cancer. Her long battle with this bully had ended.

There was my mom, lying in the middle of the ring, silent and at peace while cancer was dancing around the ring, bragging it had won. I like to believe my mom is in heaven, dancing around, bragging that she won. Chemo hadn't taken her out, Jack hadn't taken her out, suffering hadn't done it, nor had her selfish son. Even cancer hadn't taken her out ... God had taken her up.

Every second of every day cancer is baiting some people into the ring and knocking some out of it. My mom had never asked for this fight, and with God's help she never ran from it. She never said "Poor me!" Well, I'm sure she had, but that was stuff said behind closed bathroom doors. She always said, "Den, I have a real hunch God is going to heal me."

Well, that day she was finally right.

I have often thought about that poor stock boy that day, some pimple-faced sixteen-year-old who had drawn the short straw on the cleanup in aisle seven. He could have walked up to my mom, plugged his nose, and handed her a towel, telling her to clean up her own mess. He could have said, "Sorry, I make minimum wage, so they don't pay me enough to clean up your mess." But he hadn't done any of that. Instead, he'd done what Jesus had been doing for me my whole life, bending down and cleaning up my mess and not making me feel guilty for making it.

Today, people are standing in the middle of their messes in aisle seven, embarrassed and feeling more like burdens than blessings, wanting to run and hide, just wanting to die. That's what standing in messes does to people. They don't need someone to tell them they'd just made a mess. They don't need someone to protest their messes. They don't need someone making a law prohibiting any messes in aisle seven. Maybe they need someone to get down on hands and knees and say, "Mrs. Cook, I got this."

I have museums of priceless portraits of God stored in the vaults of my mind. That day, the day my Mom had been at work, I added one more picture to that collection, a pimple-faced sixteen-year-old who acted more like Jesus than a janitor that day in aisle seven.

23

T.A.D.

His name was Thomas A. Demeers, but you can call him T.A.D. He loved his initials, telling anyone who would listen, it meant Thomas A. Disciple. Nobody knows for sure, but T.A.D bragged to everyone he was named after Jesus' disciple Thomas. He was sixty something but looked forty something. His huge wire-rimmed glasses always seemed to sit lopsided on his face. He'd lived at a group home for most of his life. No one knows what happened to him; something broke a long time ago, but nobody ever told him. What he lacked intellectually was overshadowed by his self-confidence and charisma. This guy assumed everybody was his friend.

T.A.D was one the first people I met in the new church my wife and I served. He came bouncing up to me like a kangaroo on caffeine, leaking out that he played piano. He introduced himself as TAD, "That's spelled T-A-D." He told me Jesus helped him play piano and write songs. He told me how good he was and that I was pretty darn lucky to have him at this church. He proudly boasted that if I was looking for a Sunday morning special, he was the man. Plus, for the small fee of twenty bucks he would cut my grass. I said yes to both.

Within seconds he said, "You are one of my best friends."

"Thank you."

"Am I your best friend?"

"Well, umm, ahh ..."

His positive outlook saved me. "Don't worry, I will be soon."

I was warned by the church folks that when he sang, he really saaaaaang. I was also warned that he kind of made up songs on the fly. People advised me that if I had plans after church I would want to postpone them due to T.A.D.'s ability to sing all 432 verses of his made up songs.

After a few months of getting my feet wet, I decided to book T.A.D. for our opening act the following Sunday.

"T.A.D., I think I'm ready for your special this Sunday."

"I knew you would be calling me. I'm ready."

"What song are you going to play?"

"I don't know. I have to write it first."

"Do you want more time?"

"Nope, I'll be ready this Sunday," he replied.

Finally Sunday arrived. T.A.D. walked into the church in a brand-new, blue-denim jean jacket. "Are you ready for your solo, T.A.D.?"

"Wait till you see this, preacher!"

"What are you talking about?"

He spun around like a GQ model, showing off the back of his jacket; the night before he had bejeweled a bright red star on its back.

"What's the star all about?"

"Well, God told me I'm a star, and I wanted you and all the people to know that."

"Wow, can we get autographs after the service?"

He laughed and said, "Of course."

It was priceless moment I never get tired of retelling.

When it was time for his special, T.A.D. walked up to the piano with the confidence of Beethoven. Out of his pocket he pulled a folded-up piece of eight-and-a-half by eleven paper with freshly inked music and words scrambled all over it. He introduced his song, telling us all that Jesus had helped him write it. Clearing his throat, he began pounding the keys like they were nails. The only thing louder than the sound of keys was the sound of his voice. T.A.D. had no need for a microphone. You ever hear people say they are singing to the Lord? T.A.D. took it literally. If God lived in heaven, T.A.D. wanted Him and all His angel buddies to hear him. It took only a few dissident plunks of the keys to tell us composing was not his spiritual gift. I don't believe there was one note in tune the entire song, the whole long, long, long song. When his music marathon came to an end, he stood up, took a bow, and took his seat.

After the service he came up to me boasting. "See? I told you I was a star, and I have the jacket to prove it," once again turning around to display his star of fame.

Nobody in our church could sing like T.A.D. Some sang better, but nobody could sing like T.A.D. His passion for God and music was unmatched.

He would often say, "I bet ya God sure likes the Sundays I sing."

I had never met a person who was so confident God loved him. According to the world's standards, T.A.D. had so little to offer God. He had probably been talked about more than to most of his life, but somehow he never felt sorry for himself. He could spin any problem God's way. Someone once tried to pop his spiritual bubble by telling him the disciple he was named after was actually the one who had doubted Jesus. He shot back, "Who cares? At least I'm a disciple!"

Unlike T.A.D., I sometimes struggle with the way God looks at me. Because I'm a pastor I feel the pressure of being perfect, of the need to say and do everything just the way God wants it. When I blow it, which I do a lot, I apologize over and over to God, begging Him to let me out of His doghouse. At times I go into hibernation for months until I feel worthy enough to come out and face God and the world again. I hear many Christians telling others that they love God, but few that God loves them.

I would never bejewel a jean jacket with a bright, red star and tell the world, "God thinks I'm a star." I have never boasted, "I bet ya God really loves the Sundays I preach." I go home so many Sundays moping around the house, telling myself how I stunk the joint up. I'm very good at telling the whole world Jesus loves them and yet seldom tell myself that.

T.A.D. was such a wonder gift to me and our little church. I wish God would send every new pastor a T.A.D. who will pound keys, sing loud, and cut the grass all for twenty bucks. I have seldom seen anyone who has graciously accepted the cards he or she had been dealt like T.A.D. He was crazy in love with God because he knew God was crazy in love with him. He didn't have a lot to give God, but man, did he give what he had!

Some churches would never let a guy like T.A.D. pound and sing on their platforms. He would embarrass the worship team with his dissident, made-up melodies. People would poke fun of his star-studded jacket, and not many pastors would have the patience to endure 432 verses of heaven-inspired words. We like to brag we give God our best, so only the gifted voices get booked for Sunday morning slots. T.A.D.'s gift was not singing, it was loving God and letting God love him. Any time you can book a guy like that, it's worth postponing whatever you have planned after church.

Just when I thought I would never meet another saint like T.A.D. at our most recent church, an older woman walked in. I take that back—she was wheeled in. She could barely walk or see, and she has a speech problem that prevented anyone from making sense out of what she said.

In the middle of one of her first services with us, she grunted out sounds. At first I thought she was saying amen, but later I learned it meant, "I have to go to the bathroom." She too has had a few things that had broken in her life.

One Sunday I asked the church if we could sing "Jesus Loves Me" to kick off the Sunday morning service. As soon as we sang the first word she let loose. Every head in the room spun in her direction. She was practically screaming "Jesus Loves Me" in a key that had not been discovered. I stopped singing to listen to her; it was angelic-like. No, even better—it was T.A.D.-like. I could understand every word she belted out. Her face was glowing with joy I had not seen since T.A.D.'s Sunday morning specials years earlier.

I pictured God lassoing His angels, shutting down heaven for a few minutes, bragging "Look at that lady sing to me. She believes I love her, and that makes Me really happy."

His name was Thomas A. Demeers, but you could call him T.A.D. Life was pretty simple to him. When he pounded the keys in or out of tune, God was happy. When he belted out a scrabble-board full of made-up words, God was happy. When he modeled a star-studded jean jacket, God was happy. When he cut grass for twenty bucks, he knew God was happy. He believed whatever he did, God was happy with him, and the Devil himself couldn't talk him out of it. But that makes sense, right? After all, he was named after one of Jesus' disciples.

24

Black Socks

I worked in a factory for over ten years before God called me to be a pastor. I thought He had the wrong number because I didn't like pastors. What I mean is, I didn't like the image many pastors portrayed. In my naivete I thought they worked only one day a week, really an hour a week. They all had closets stuffed with fancy-dancy pinstriped suits, shiny cuff links, and matching black wing tips. I reminded God I didn't have a suit, so how could I possibly be a pastor? I thought they had no connection to the real world and always seemed to be selling miracles for money when they weren't golfing. After months of wrestling with God, He won, which at the time implied I lost. I quit my job, sold my junk, got a black suit, and off to college I went.

After squeezing a four-year degree into five and a half years, I finally graduated from a Christian college and was ready to bump Billy Graham out of the way so I could save the world. Yep, it's official—Dennis James Cook is a bona fide pastor who now can marry and bury legally. I was standing with a piece of white paper, a black gown, and a funny square cap to prove it. People started calling me Pastor Dennis. Wow, that sure was a lot nicer than some of the names my buddies back home called me. One of the first times someone called me pastor in public he had to repeat it fifty-seven times before I realized he was talking to me.

If you would have asked me anything about life I would have given you an answer (maybe after having googled it). Life was very black and white in those early days; I could diagnose your problem and search the Bible, books, and the Internet for quick spiritual remedies. I can't tell you how many "five steps to this and twelve steps to that" my degree gave me permission to prescribe to the broken. After graduation I was soliciting God as to whom He wanted me to fix first. You had questions? I had answers.

I remember one of my first days on the job, sitting in my new office, staring at my phone, waiting for my first problem to fix. The phone finally rang. A family friend was desperately crying, "Dennis, can you stop by my house?"

"Sure! What's up?"

"I'll tell you when you get here."

I diagnosed the distress in his voice; I thought he was going to be my first patient to patch up for Jesus.

When I got to his house he seemed to be somewhat dazed and confused. His eyes were wet and red from crying, and his beard hadn't seen a razor in days. I asked him what the problem was.

The words slowly dribbled out of his mouth. "My wife of thirty-one years is dead."

I was caught a little off-guard by this; it was a little trickier than I thought my first house call would be. I took a deep breath and tried to remember what my textbooks had offered on death and dying. Oh yeah, I remember a question from my psychology 101 class.

"So how does this make you feel?"

"What do you mean, how does this make me feel?"

"Well, how do you feel about your wife dying?" I explained.

"I feel this is some heavenly hoax, a mistake. I feel like someone has plunged a hand through my chest and ripped out my heart and left me for dead. I feel like a few days ago I was the luckiest guy in the world, and today I can't feel anything. I can still smell her perfume on the pillow and don't want to wash it. All morning I've buried my face in her pillowcase, almost suffocating myself, trying to breathe in one more memory."

I was clearly in way in over my degree at this point; I should have 'fessed up, pleaded the fifth, and prayed. But instead I stayed in character and tried acting spiritual.

"Well, have you asked God for help? The Bible tells us He is our ever-present help in times of trouble."

"No, Dennis, I have not asked for God's help. What good would it do? My wife is dead. How am I going to get through this?"

"Well, you need to believe that greater is He who is in you than he who is in the world ... that's in the Bible somewhere." I tossed in a few extra psalms as a sedative free of charge, hoping something would ease his pain.

Ignoring all my biblical counsel, he explained, "All I do is cry all day and night. I can't stop crying. Every time I close my eyes I see her, and when I open them she's gone. I'm wishing I could shut my eyes and never open them again. I've lost my reason to live."

I recalled a verse I memorized in college on this type of deep sorrow, "Weeping may last for a night, but joy comes in the morning. I'm so sorry for what you're going through, but you have to know God is good."

"Well, He sure doesn't feel so good right now, and I'm very angry with God for twiddling his thumbs while my wife was dying."

I think I lobbed him some Christian comeback along the lines of, "We don't put our faith in feelings but in the Word of God."

I was pretty excited how God was using me and my degree in such a powerful way. I felt to this point he had had tough questions and I had some good answers from the Word of God. I admit I was not real familiar with this house-call stuff then, but I was giving him a perfect dose of truth and grace. I was thinking he and I were running out of things to say and was ready to dismiss myself.

Before I could exit this delicate situation he walked into their bedroom and plopped down on the edge of their king-sized bed. I followed him, pulling up a seat next to him and pondering his next question and my next answer. He was staring at the floor. I followed his eyes but saw nothing.

"What you are staring at?"

Without saying a word he slowly bent over and picked up one of his wife's black socks off the floor. He gently held it in front of my face and looked at me with tears rushing out. "You seem to have had an answer for everything I've said since you got here. I have just one more question, Dennis. What do you want me to do with her black sock?"

"What do you mean, what do you do with her black sock?"

"What do I do with her black sock? Do I throw it in the dirty clothes? Do I throw it in the trash? Do I give it to the Salvation Army? Do I frame it and put it on the wall?"

"I don't know what to do with her black sock." Then it hit me. In all my theology, psychology, and counseling classes no one had ever taught me what to do with the sock of a widower's dead wife. I was feeling pretty cruddy for trying to jam the whole Bible into his open wound because it made it bleed only more. I doubt even Google could satisfy his thirst for answers. He had questions, and I had answers but no solutions; I sadly didn't even pray with him. I was so concerned about saying the right thing that I missed doing the right thing, listen.

All my education, square hat, and framed piece of paper decorating my wall seemed to mean nothing as I sat on the corner of that bed. Why hadn't I seen the black sock on the floor? Maybe it was because my wife was still living. Maybe it was because I'd been too busy trying to repair what no degree had the power to do. A degree will never fill a hole that death randomly dug. A degree will never heal a single man sleeping in a double bed. A degree will never tell a widower what to do with a black sock.

Every verse I gave him was true. God is greater … He is our ever-present help … Joy does come in the morning. But the real question was what morning? As a rookie pastor I thought my job was to diagnose people's problems, open the Bible, prescribe a few verses like aspirins, and call it good.

I still believe God and the Bible are the only hopes in times of trouble, but I add just one more thing: when life knocks the wind out of people, they look for someone, anyone, who's willing to sit with them long enough to catch their breath. They look for people who would never dare prescribe Bible verses on sorrow without tears. They look for people to cry with them more than for them. They look for people willing to sit long enough to figure out what to do with a black sock and the broken person holding it.

If you've paid attention to half of what you've just read, you understand I blew my rookie visit. God did help this man in spite of the fumbling of my faith. I hoped for a little redemption by writing his story to help prepare the next person staring at a black sock.

I wrote this story camped out next to the only working plug at a coffee shop. As I was ready to plunk down the final sentence of this story I realized a wife who had lost her husband was called widow, but I wasn't sure what you called a man who had lost his wife. I quizzed an older man sitting next to me.

"A widower. I know this because I lost my wife," he said without hesitation.

I thought How ironic; I'm writing a story about a spiritual test I failed decades ago, and here's an unexpected chance for a retake. I took a deep breath. Don't blow this by prescribing a mouthful of religious placebos.

I asked him his name and if he wanted to talk. He floated back to a place and time he could see when he closed his eyes. He smiled and bragged about his wife and marriage as if she had been sitting next to us. I'd dealt with so many marriages that had lost their spark. Even though his wife was gone, the fire was still burning. It was so cool to hear a man in love and wanting the whole world to know it.

I felt this was not a coincidence, so I asked him if he was willing to read my short story about a black sock. He looked at me, confused. I guess that made sense. How many times have you gone into a coffee shop and had a stranger ask you to read his short story about a sock? He halfheartedly agreed to read the story. I slid my computer next to his cold coffee.

He started to read it, and tears fell as freely as my friend's had twenty years previously. I remained silent, no verses, no psych 101 babble, no answering unasked questions. We just looked at each other; neither of us knew what to say next.

He slid his wooden chair a bit closer to mine, whispering, "My wife has been dead for four years. On November twenty-first it will be five. It's weird, and I still don't know what to do with the black sock."

He confessed his weak faith, and that was followed by a spontaneous eruption of how he was still mad at God for not answering his desperate plea for help. He looked at me and shared as though it were common sense, "You know, every person who has lost someone has a black sock, and none of us really knows what to do with it."

I nodded. "Yes sir, you're so right."

I asked him if I could pray for him. He said please. I prayed a simple prayer I had been preparing for twenty years.

"Dear God, help my new friend's heart heal, and be close to him, amen." He was so grateful that someone had written his story in black and white. I invited myself to meet him again for coffee someday.

He smiled, saying, "Here's the miracle. I live in California, and I'm here in Michigan on business. I was driving by this coffee shop and thought I should pull in and grab a cup of coffee. I'm so glad I did. It proved God has not forgotten about me. It proves He still loves me even if I haven't found a place for my own black sock yet."

"Yes God does love you because I hate coffee and I'm writing in a coffee shop."

We both chuckled, agreeing this had been a setup by God Himself.

Before heading west, he asked if he could insert a few sentences in my book to you, its readers. I agreed, knowing it would be far better than anything I could have written because my wife is still wearing her black socks.

"Dennis, tell them healing is slow; really slow, and sometimes too slow. Tell them God does not abandon us at our weakest places in life. Tell them sometimes with enough love, patience, and God's grace we will find a place for our black sock. Some try to ignore it ... Some try to throw it away ... and some frame it ... but none of us forget it. Sometimes I have to scream out loud 'God is good' even if every bone in my body disagrees."

He began to cry again not because he'd lost his wife but because God had found him that day. That was incredible! This guy felt that God loved him, and I hadn't prescribed any solutions; I had simply let him read a story that reminded him he was not the only one holding a black sock.

I have sat with hundreds of broken people who don't know what to do with their black socks. I have witnessed oceans of tears splashed on the floors of those who had had their hearts ripped out without their permission. I don't have enough fingers and toes to count the people who are mad at God for not coming through as they thought He should have. Every day we pass hundreds of people tethered to their black socks just looking for someone to stop long enough to listen to their stories.

When I first started ministry I thought degrees, good grades, books, seminars and Google could fix just about anything and one phone call and a black sox proved me wrong.

25

Car Alarm

He strutted into the church with hair as long as Jesus and dyed a color you could find only in a box of crayons. His faded blue jeans had tailored holes in both knees, which he had paid extra for, and a T-shirt with something stamped on it that most church folks wouldn't endorse. He had a habit of folding his bronze locks behind his ears and exposing his matching earrings in the process. He obviously didn't get the memo that Jesus wouldn't wear holey jeans, unholy T-shirts, and earrings. It was his first Sunday in church, and he was as spiritually green as grass in July. He'd heard this was the place to come if you needed some fixing.

His unique fashion style was a magnet that drew the eyes and the criticism of a few of the "mature in Christ." Whispers began to slither through the church pews like snakes through a garden. It seemed that some were not too keen on his less-than-godly attire. Some brave souls took it upon themselves to investigate why he would come to church looking like some leftover hippie from the sixties. These gentle giants of the faith were kind enough to help Jesus out by inquiring if he would kindly snip his hair, wear a tie, and unplug his bling. Due to his youth and naivete in the "ways of the Lord" they were more than willing to steer him back in the right direction.

Poor kid was clueless as to what the big stink was all about. Why were so many strangers so concerned about his hair and earrings? His logic: "Hey, I wore clothes, didn't I?" No one asked him his name, but you can bet they gave him a few. This was not quite what he had expected his first trip to church would be like.

A few weeks ago something happened that dragged me back decades to that memory. I wanted to do something nice for my wife, who is not known for keeping vehicles clean inside or out. I decided to steal her car for an hour and surprise her with a sparkling makeover. I drove to one of those do-it-yourself places where one hundred and fifty-two quarters just about gets the job done if you don't rinse. I decided to break the bank and do her interior as well.

I was almost done with her car and my good deed for the day when I must have accidently bumped something. The car alarm started blaring and making a scene. I hit the panic button to make the noise go away, but nothing happened. I poked it harder. Nothing. Not knowing what to do, I gently slapped the dash. Nothing. I punched the dash with a right hook. The alarm blared on. I smacked the steering wheel, turned the car on, and pumped the brakes a thousand times. Zip. I tapped, punched, and smacked anything within reach to get that foolish thing to quiet down. I was so desperate I yelled at the stupid car alarm to shut up, which did absolutely nothing.

As you may have already guessed, I know nothing about cars. When going on one of my first dates with my now-wife Heidi I saw a little red light flicker on the dash. The car began to sputter and limp the farther we drove. I took a chance that the red light meant it needed oil. I pulled into the gas station and acted as if I knew what I was doing, trying to impress my lady. I walked in and told the girl I needed oil.

"What kind?"

"Ahh, car oil of course!" She pointed me to the oil aisle, and I did the "eenie-meenie-miney-moe" thing and grabbed something with "oil" on the label.

I popped the hood and started to investigate the red-light dilemma. I was not real familiar with under-the-hood stuff; my job as a kid had been to hold the flashlight. I kept staring at the engine and all its gadgets, wires, and cables. After a few minutes of pretending I knew what I was doing I shut the hood and slid back into the car like everything was cool. I pitched the full can of oil into the backseat and said, "That should do it."

Heidi looked at me. "You couldn't find the dipstick, could you?"

"Nope." I think she laughed for the next three and a half days.

Meanwhile, back at the car wash, my disgruntled alarm had by then summoned an audience. I was embarrassed as people were pointing and chuckling at all my pounding and punching. I was running out of things to hit and holler at. I even tried to get spiritual: "Dear God, if it's in Your will, if You would please make this dimwitted alarm stop beeping now, I would be most grateful." Nothing. I think even He had started to point and chuckle.

After hours and hours—okay, minutes—of my wife's car putting on a concert for the community, I noticed a man rummaging through a trash container for cans. Each time I looked his way he was staring at me. But hey, who wasn't? My patience was slowly evaporating with every dissident note screeching out from under the hood. I was minutes away from giving up and driving home alarm on and all. The man sifting for empties started to circle my car like a vulture. Okay, I thought, this is odd. It's one thing to make fun of me from a distance, but to circle the car gaping into my windows is another. After a few laps he stopped about four feet from my door, just staring at me. I gave him the What the heck ya' doin' look. He didn't get it and continued his piercing gaze.

After a few minutes he twirled his hand in circles, sign language for roll down your window. I was looking around my car for spare change to give him before rolling down my window. I grabbed a clump of quarters, willing to fill his empty pockets to get him to mosey on down the road.

I rolled down my window and asked, "What is it you need?" preparing to give him some money.

With the sincerity of a monk he asked, "Hey, mister, do you know your car alarm is on?"

I didn't know how to respond; well, I knew how I wanted to respond.

"Of course I know my alarm is on. It's been pitching a fit for the last hour."

He smiled and said, "Good, just wanted you to know," and he shuffled off to his next stop.

I didn't know whether to laugh or scream. Really? All that staring, walking, and twirling of the hand to tell me my alarm was on? The more I thought of his obvious analysis the more I laughed. He had been so proud of his diagnosis of my dilemma. I believed he thought he was helping me.

Just as magical as the alarm started it stopped. I rolled out slightly embarrassed thinking this sure would make a good story someday.

Nowadays, each time I hear a car alarm sound off, I want to walk around the car, peek in, motion to the poor driver to roll down the window, and mention that the alarm is on just to see what my face must have looked like.

The following Sunday in church I shared that story with our people. They too laughed with me; at least I think they were laughing with me.

The more I thought of this story the more I thought of the hippie. He'd walked into a strange church thinking it was the right thing to do. It was not that church was his first option; it was his last. He never tried to hide his brokenness. He walked in with his alarm signaling to everyone willing to pay attention that something was seriously wrong but that it was not the outside that needed fixing.

In my opinion the church has mastered the art of polishing up the outside of folks before the inside. It is so much easier and faster to make a person look like a glossy Christian than to wait on God to do His thing. It's so much easier to tell people, "Hey, your alarm is on." What they don't realize or won't is that everyday people wake up and go to bed with the ringing of what's wrong with them blaring in their heads.

After months of prodding and having been poked fun of, the hippie finally gave up and gave in. He visited a barber, bought dress pants, roped a tie around his neck, and unplucked his earrings. When he showed up to church the following Sunday you would have thought the pope had walked in. The saints cheered with glee over his squeaky-clean exterior makeover. The news sprinted through the church pew by pew.

"Hey did you see who cut his hair and unplugged his earrings? Yes, the beatnik has finally broken free of the sixties."

People poured piles and piles of praise on him, reminding him how pleased God was with his new, sanitized look. They let him know God gives us His best when we give Him our best. Some were showing him off like a prized pup on one of those ESPN dog shows.

"Why did you do it?" I asked him after the service.

"I just wanted them to love me. I wanted to fit in," he said with his chin plunged into his chest.

"So let me ask you, did it turn out like you thought? Do you feel more loved this week than last?"

"No, I feel less loved. I came here to be loved, not laughed at. I stayed here thinking the looks and laughs would stop. I wanted them to help me on the inside, but all they could see or wanted to see was the outside. Now that I changed my outside I don't like my inside. This doesn't feel like I thought it was going to feel."

He quietly moped around the church for a few more months and drifted back to wherever short-haired earringless ex-hippies go. He was just one more victim in a long line of broken people who limp into church only to be told, "Hey, do you know your alarm's on?"

I saw him a few years later. He'd grown out his hair, slipped back into his jeans, and plugged his earrings back in. No one really missed him, and he didn't miss them. It's funny that when he left the church they both thought they had won.

26
Hockey Fights

A friend of mine has some real anger issues. Wherever he goes, fights follow. Almost every time we meet, he has a story about a fight that had broken out right in front of him and he just had to jump in. His face is very familiar with bloody lips and black eyes. This guy's life has more drama than any ten episodes of "Days of Our Lives."

I personally am not too fond of pain—giving or receiving. I've inadvertently passed this sheepish trait to my younger daughter. We were driving one day, and I encouraged her to take more risks in her life.

With no hesitation she spit back, "Dad, if there's any chance of getting hurt, I ain't doin' it!" She elaborated, "Why would I do anything that would cause me pain?"

It was then I realized we don't always have to teach someone something to teach someone something. Over the years she'd picked up on my detours of things that could cause bloody lips and black eyes. I thought I had the perfect pacifist résumé to counsel my friend with his anger issues. I invited him to a Detroit Red Wings hockey game to give him some free tutoring tips. Before going I brushed up a bit on what the Bible has to say about anger. I was very confident "Dr. Cook" could fix his fighting flaws with one session.

We had about an hour's drive to the game that night that provided a great window of time for me to teach him how to get trouble to quit keeping tabs on him. I educated him that the Bible says we should pray for our enemies, not punch them. It seemed my wisdom was taking root; I felt very confident about our one-hour session on anger management. I asked him, "Does this make sense?" I interpreted his nod as a yes.

We walked into the game, and our tickets landed us in standing room only about halfway up the arena. It was a great game full of a sports fan's holy trinity: fights, Ball Park franks, and screaming at the refs. But between the second and third periods a slightly sauced fan began to get a bit rowdy. He started to yell out four-letter words in front of the kids standing nearby; my buddy didn't think it was right. I could see the mercury in his thermostat rising.

"Hey, Dennis, think I should tell that loud mouth to keep his big trap shut?"

"No, no! Don't you remember our little chat on anger and praying?"

"I'd prefer to do this my way."

I gave him a bonus Bible verse free of charge. "No, God's ways are always better than our ways.'"

He calmed down, and I thought, Wow, this Bible stuff works! After patting myself on the back I leaned back up against the wall. Just as the third period began, the oversized man barged his way in next to me carrying fourteen beers. He kept elbowing me farther and farther out of my standing-room-only spot without saying excuse me. He began to screech out obscenities that would make your ear hairs curl and give this book an R rating. If I can smell your Bud Breath bro, we may be a bit too close. I briefly thought about relocating. But these are our seats, and I ain't moving.

As he was chanting off-key "Let's go Red Wings," when one of his fourteen beers accidently spilled on my brand-new Adidas sweatsuit. I glanced his way, expecting him to say, "Hey dude, I'm sorry." But he stared at me like it was my fault, while any jury in Michigan would have unanimously confirmed it had not been.

Okay, this is just a test. Be calm, Dennis. Your "student" is watching how you'll respond. I took a deep breath, looked this goon in the eyes, and gave him a fake smile to let him know how nice I was. I wanted him to know my faith was stronger than his beer flinging. Sure enough, my buddy was watching every twitch of my face.

I was quite pleased with the exhibition of kindness I had displayed for this disorderly fan. Then out of nowhere the guy took his beer and poured it all down the front of my new sweatsuit. It was now my thermostat that was about to explode and spew mercury everywhere!

I looked at him and asked, "What in the heck did you do that for?"

The ape glared down at me and mocked, "Oh, I'm sorry! Did I get your precious, little sweatsuit wet?"

"Did you get it wet? It's soaked, you jerk!" Okay, I didn't say "jerk" because that wouldn't have been very Christian like, but I did think it.

"I'm sorry. Let me give you some money to buy a new one."

"Yeah, you better pay for it!"

He set down his keg and reached into his wallet and pulled out two bucks, laughing. "That should just about cover it."

I was boiling! I don't care if Goliath is your twin! You and I are going to go at it right now. I'm not going to take it anymore! Even Jesus would give this heathen a piece of his mind and a right hook. Probably not, but in the heat of the moment we always like to drag Jesus to our side. We were ready to throw off the gloves and face off. I didn't care what the Bible said or if I won or lost; a guy can take only so much.

Before I was about to get thrashed by this bully, my buddy interrupted. "Stop, Dennis! What about the Bible lesson? What about that 'praying for our enemies' stuff?"

I was foaming at the mouth, ready to fight Goliath with or without a slingshot, but my friend stepped in and said, "Let's go stand somewhere else."

"No! This is my spot!" I folded my arms, gritted my teeth, and stood there, baptized in beer, smelling like a brewery.

Thankfully, the only fights that night ended up being on the ice. Trust me; my buddy got a kick out of that night. For over an hour on our ride home all I heard was, "Hey! What an awesome night! You taught me about anger all the way there, and it was you with the anger issues. That's funny, Dennis, isn't it?"

I tried to convince him that was not who I normally was.

"It was tonight!"

I just bit my lip till it bled with humiliation.

What I learned was that my friend never asked me to tutor him in a class about anger management. I just saw the damage it was doing to him and his family and tossed in my tips. I assumed because I had brilliantly diagnosed his problem he wanted me to fix it. It's very difficult to offer a solution to someone who doesn't feel he or she has a problem. He felt he was fine; he just wanted to hang out, eat Ball Parks, watch fights, and yell at the refs.

I so wanted to teach him a lesson I hadn't fully learned myself. I had looked at his anger and had thought I could fix years of bloody lips and black eyes with a few verses and a hockey game. Too often we Christians look at other people's problems and think, Oh, that's an easy fix. We tell them, "If you would just read this book … If you would just listen to hours and hours of sermons … If you would just go to the next popular conference on "How to Be a Better Christian in Seven Easy Steps." Or we give them the mother lode of advice to beat all advice: "If you would just do what the Bible says, your life would be super-duper, just like mine!" I think the reason so many people do not choose to be Christians is because they don't want to turn out like the person trying to save them.

All I had had to do that night was stand five feet to the left or the right, and all would have been good in hockey town and heaven. Instead, my pride got the best of me. God gave me the same test that night I was giving my friend, but he passed. Me? Well, all I got was a soaked suit, two bucks, and a bloody lip.

27

Hundred-Dollar Steak

I was being swallowed up by a very comfy chair in the gold-painted lobby of the Ritz Carlton in Washington, D.C. My friend and I were attending some meetings downtown for the week, and he asked if I wanted to tag along to meet an ol' buddy of his. As I watched the cars pull into the Ritz I realized many of them had cost more than the trailer I was living in at the time. The fancy clothes the people were wearing gave me a hint that this place might cost a drop more than the Motel 8s I was used to bunking in. I looked down at my socks and realized they were not matching. Again. I tried to shimmy my jeans down to cover up my sock gaffe. I looked down and saw that I'd been toting an empty, twelve-ounce, plastic Coke bottle in my pocket. (Hey, that was worth ten cents!)

I had no crested sports jacket, no pleated pants, no tie, no shimmering cuff links, so I was feeling more out of place than a nun at a heavy metal concert; it was one of the swankiest hotel lobbies I'd ever been in. Ten minutes earlier I'd never even thought about our modest mobile home. Ten minutes earlier I'd liked me and the way I dressed even if I was wearing one black and one blue sock. But being round all this D.C. money made me feel a bit underdressed and outclassed.

My buddy's friend showed up, and we slipped into the lounge for a drink. I ordered a Coke, and his friend ordered something with Coke in it. His friend dressed as if he'd stepped straight out of a GQ magazine ad. I put my mouth in park to not embarrass myself or my friend.

Whether it was intentional or not, it slipped out that the guy had worked for the White House doing something very important. He and my buddy volleyed conversation back and forth, everything from politics to poetry, for about an hour. This guy's a genius! The kind of guy who would hold his own on "Jeopardy." After an hour of random chatter they decided it was time for dinner and asked for the tab. I peeked at the price for my Coke and was shocked; eight bucks for a Coke the size of a thimble!

The three of us scooted into a steak place around the corner. I was informed this was a place where the Washington elite mingle and make deals. Feeling a bit self-conscious, I wondered how many senators were wearing mismatched socks and living in mobile homes. My guess was zero. We were ushered to our table and given a menu with our names printed on top. How'd they do that? This is so cool! This place is going in my journal as the nicest restaurant I've ever eaten at, and I haven't swallowed even one bite yet!

Everything looked appetizing, but I noticed there were no prices following the food choices and no dollar menu. I whispered to my friend, "Hey, how do we know how much stuff costs?"

My friend chuckled. "If people have to ask, this may be the wrong restaurant. Don't worry, order what you want—it's on me."

I'm telling you it was weird to order food with no idea how much it cost. So I ordered a side of beef, potatoes, veggies, salad, and a gallon of Heinz Ketchup to baptize my steak in.

I let them catch up on old times as I eyeballed what priceless dessert was begging for my attention. Then I overheard something that interrupted my sugar fantasy and grabbed my ear. My friend's friend confessed out of the blue, "This life really stinks."

You got to be kidding me! You have a job most people can only dream of; you work at the White House, where the president lives. The cost of your suit could put both my teenage daughters through college. You have a house in a gated neighborhood. You can eat at any restaurant you want, even ones without prices. From where I'm sitting, brother, you got it good; you're living the American dream.

He sunk his chin into his loosened tie, leaking out the ugly details of a fresh divorce.

"I'm losing it all. She's found someone else. I'm losing my wife, my kids, and our house. I'm living in a rented apartment by myself right down the street. I swear I never saw it coming. I mean, we didn't have the perfect marriage, but divorce? No way! I worked hard giving them everything they wanted, and this is my reward? Divorce? I don't get it! Do you know what it feels like to drive by my house and see some guy replacing me, pushing my kids on the swing set I built? Do you know what it feels like watching some guy sitting on my riding mower cutting what used to be my grass? Do you know what it feels like to drive by at eleven at night and knowing some guy is sleeping in my bed with my wife? My life is pathetic. I can afford to eat hundred-dollar steaks, but I'm eating them alone. I'm losing it all, and no amount of money can buy it back."

He was having a nervous breakdown in one of the nicest restaurants in the world. My friend and I had been caught off-guard in our front-row seats watching the crumbling of the American dream. He continued to dump his hurt all over us as if we were his therapists. We listened to him without interruption for what seemed hours. He stopped talking and started crying.

Wow, had I read this sharply dressed man wrong. I'd been thinking about how I wished I had his life and the privileges it afforded him. I was jealous of his money and his mansion. I could never stay at the Ritz or graze at a place like I was in without having won the lottery. I'd been duped by the suit, tie, cuff links, and cash. I was sitting next to a man who was contemplating ending it because he had lost what no amount of money could buy back, his family.

He had finally realized his money couldn't buy him one more pushing of his kids on a swing, that his money couldn't buy him one more trip around the yard on his John Deere, that his money couldn't buy his way back into his bedroom or one night of peace. His money could buy only a rented apartment, an eight-dollar Coke, and a hundred-dollar steak he had to eat alone. He wished at that point he had spent more time at his house rather than the White House. He was willing to trade all his wealth, power, and prestige for one more chance to go home.

I sat silent for hours, knowing it was time to speak, but I didn't know what to say. I fumbled through a few Christian clichés, but they all seemed more like bumper stickers than life preservers. Out of sheer lack of nothing to say I asked him if I could pray for him. Before he could answer I closed my eyes and prayed the best half-minute prayer my heart allowed. I prayed he would see that God loves him, and I assured him He would not abandon him in his time of crisis.

When I said amen, I looked over and saw the White House worker bawling over his hundred-dollar steak. After a few minutes of nobody saying anything, in fear of screwing up the moment he confessed, "I'm in my sixties, and nobody in my entire life has ever prayed with me face-to-face."

"What do you mean?" I asked.

"I have never in my entire life had anyone stop to pray with me in person. I've been in and out of churches, hearing religious prayers fly over my head, but never has a person stopped to pray with me face-to-face."

I was more shocked over this depressing sentence than I had been over the eight-dollar Coke and the hundred-dollar steak.

He politely replied, "Thank you. That was a very nice thing you did there, praying with me."

It got me thinking how many people, whether they stay at the Ritz or in trailer parks, whether they have matching socks or mixed, whether they're GQ or J.C. Penney people, have never had one person stop and pray for them. I don't know if he ever got to push his daughter, cut his grass, or sleep with his wife again. I don't know if he still works at the White House or at a Walmart, but I do know for those thirty seconds He felt God's love.

I think people are starving for folks to stop and pray with them, not at them. If I had seen this guy on TV I would have judged him Democrat or Republican, pro-choice or pro-life, liberal or conservative based on the policies he promoted. The Red try to convert the Blue and vice versa, trying to convince us the world would be a better place with their hue in charge. I would have thought he was just another one of those rich politicians who ate hundred-dollars steaks and stuck the American public with the bill. Until that dinner I would never have thought of a politician as a broken man looking for someone to see beyond his suit and his steak. I never would have thought of him as a man ready it to end it all just because he had lost it all. I would have looked at him and said, "There's a sharp-dressed man living out the American dream."

I learned two very valuable lessons that night: God can use a guy who has two different-colored socks, and what the heck good is a hundred-dollar steak if you have to eat it alone?

28

Walking on Water

After church one hot, Michigan summer Sunday my five-year-old daughter came up and verbally tackled me with, "Dad! Dad! Guess what!"

"What, honey?"

She gushed, "This guy in the Bible got out of his boat and walked on water, and guess what? He didn't sink!"

I played it coy, as if I'd never heard the story. I leaned in.

"What was the guy's name?

"Paul or Peter, I'm not sure, but I think it started with P." She could not get over that somebody had actually walked on water and hadn't sunk. I guess I'd read and reread that story so many times I'd almost forgotten how cool it really was.

We had a church picnic in the park right after the service. As we were corralling our picnic tables, all the kids scattered to play on one of those wooden playthings as big as a small city. It was the perfect day for family, friends, and food.

As we were sitting down to eat, I noticed someone was missing. It took a few minutes, but it hit me my little girl was absent! I desperately scanned the park for a three-and-a-half foot runaway. I saw her walking to the river next to the park. I sprinted over to intercept her before she slipped down the rocky bank.

I caught up with her. "Mackenzie! You can't just walk away without telling someone!"

She looked at me as if she hadn't heard a word. She kept on marching toward the water. I increased the volume a few decibels. "Mackenzie! Stop!"

She walked to the edge of the river, staring down at the water racing below her. I asked, "What are you doing?"

"I'm ready, Dad. Yep, I think I'm ready."

"Honey, we're all ready—ready to eat and waiting on you, so let's go."

With a big gulp of air she said, "Nope. I'm ready to walk on water, Dad. This is my time."

I politely tried redirecting her misguided enthusiasm back to the picnic table, but she was not moving. Having forgotten our earlier conversation, I asked, "Where did you get such a crazy idea?"

"At church this morning. In the sermon, remember?"

"Oh, that Peter thing. Well, honey, that's just a story from the Bible a long time ago. Mackenzie, God didn't mean for little girls to literally try to walk on water."

I have been stumped many times in my brief pastoral career, but nothing like what happened next. She looked me in the eyes and asked, "Dad, do you believe I can walk on water?"

Now I gulped for air and an answer. If I told her no, that would have gone against everything she'd learned just hours ago in church. But worse, if I said yes and she sunk, that just may have been too much for a five-year-old's faith to handle.

I was going to have to strap her on my back like a sack of potatoes and retreat or take the rocky descent of faith to the water's edge with her. She interrupted my paternal dilemma by repeating her question. "So do you believe I can walk on water?"

Just then I felt God taking pity on me and dropping some Solomon-like wisdom on my head.

"Mackenzie, if God wants you to walk on water, you'll walk on water."

That was all she needed to uncage her monster-like faith. I swallowed her little hand in mine. Together we began our rocky descent to the water that would soon test both of our faiths. Well, there she was, all three and a half feet of her, two inches away from testing out a 2,000-year-old Bible story. She asked, "Should I keep my sandals on or take them off?"

I thought, I don't think that matters. "Your choice."

She flipped off her right sandal and was ready to walk on water. The moment of truth arrived. She gave me one last glance full of fear and faith. She slowly maneuvered her right foot, hovering over the rapid waters. After a few minutes of second guessing, she gently lowered her foot to the top of the water as I held my breath praying, "I think she can, I think she can …"

She smiled as her foot was resting on the water trickling over her tiny arch. Then she cautiously shifted her weight to her right foot and sploosh—she sank like a rock. I quickly snatched her and reeled her and her reckless faith in to shore.

I was thinking she was going to blame God, me, or the church for false advertising. I was going through a biblical Rolodex for wisdom to give a five-year-old who had just failed at her maiden voyage of water walking. This time Solomon left me hanging. So I was just ready to give her an "Atta girl" pep talk for trying what so few wouldn't, and the coolest thing happened.

She had this mammoth smile on her face, saying, "Daddy, if it's okay with you, I think I'll walk on water another day. Let's eat."

"Yes, let's try another day."

I will never forget that day and the lessons it had taught me: you'll never walk on water unless you try, and sometimes you won't walk on water even if you do try.

I used to be a water walker; it's just that I have sunk and have swallowed so many gallons of water that I seldom try anymore. I would have bet my house at times that certain things were God's will for me to do, but weeks later, sploosh! At times I've done my best to try to help others only to end up hurting them. Sploosh! There have been times I've followed a dream only to have it turn into a nightmare. Sploosh!

But what's weird is after a full résumé of sinking I can't ever remember saying to God, myself, or others, "Oh, no problem. I'll just walk on water another day." The more I sink, the more I blame God, myself, and the church for my splooshes. The more I sink, the less I try to walk on water. The more I sink, the more I say there will be no another day.

The world has fleets of dry, fearful people clinging to the boat and hoping not to get wet, hoping to play it safe, hoping to stay dry till they die. They will religiously stand before God and brag, "I never sank."

He will say with pity, "That's too bad ... There were so many things worth getting wet for, but you missed them all by clinging to the boat."

I've made a comfortable living by staying safe and dry inside the boat for most of my life. I've convinced myself that God can use me better dry than wet. But looking back, what bothers me most about that summer day was that in my mind I just knew she would sink. I knew she had zero chances of walking on water. I now wish for even just a few seconds of that day back. I wouldn't have played it coy, blowing off her childlike faith. I wish I would have forgotten about eating and instead flipped off my sandals and said, "Hey, honey, let's go walk on water together or sink together, but either way our feet are getting wet." I should have been leading her to the water, not having her lead me. I wrongly thought by not letting her try to walk on water I was protecting her faith, but I now see I was only hurting it.

That breathtaking, miraculous story of Peter jumping out of the boat and walking on water is just that for many people, including me: a story. It's one of those stories we've become so familiar with that we don't know what it means anymore. As a pastor, I can tell you what the story of water walking says, but it took a five-year-old to show me what it actually means.

29
Just Sat There

Every now and then I get the chance to sneak out of our church and speak at another. A pastor will ask me to do a series of sermons on a particular topic they feel will help pump up their flock. Once I was asked to speak for about five nights. It's always fun but always an uphill challenge to preach to a group of strangers.

I enjoyed the week of meeting new people and hearing their stories. Out of all the people I met that week one woman stood out. She was pushing fifty but dressed like twenty-nine and holding. Her outfit was matching from head to toe. Plenty of gold jewelry draped around her neck and wrists. Each night she clearly won the award for best dressed. But it was not what she wore that caused her to stand out. She stood out because she just sat there all week long glued to her pew. She employed the same seat each service, six rows back, on the right side of the church.

If I said a joke, she just sat there. If we sang a fast song, she just sat there. If we sang a slow song, she just sat there. By the end of the week I was getting a complex that maybe it was me to blame for her impersonation of a fence post. Maybe my preaching was too long, too short, too boring. My preaching has been known to put babies and folks over seventy who have missed their naps to sleep, but she was neither. No matter what I said or did she just sat there, staring through me.

On the last night of my speaking I opened up the service by asking what God had done over our last week. Some stood and said how this or that verse had helped them see God more clearly. Some recited a story I'd shared that mirrored their lives and sparked their faith. Some said it had helped them be better parents and people. Some even said they had accepted Jesus that week. Most of the time such praise can put me in a good mood for months. It was a memorable last night of people standing and telling stories of what God had done.

But that one woman just sat there as frozen as a Popsicle through it all.

Lady, didn't you just hear what I heard? Didn't you just hear your people accepting the Lord? They're going to heaven! Yeehaw! Hallelujah! Praise the Lord!

Nope, nothing. She just sat there.

Why would you show up all week if you were going to just sit there like a rock? I can think of thousands of better things to do than listen to me each night.

Well, I did the best I could to finish strong. I did a short little ditty on grace, always a safe way to close out a week of preaching. That way, if I had stunk up the joint earlier in the week I could always use a bit of what I was preaching, grace. It was not that deep of a message with a lot of clever points. It was not a sermon at the end of which I would pour a dump truck of guilt on them for not being perfect. It was very simple; I pitched a few words their way about how grace can find us even when we can't find it.

I concluded the service and the whole week with a robust amen. All I could think about after the long week was going home and squeezing the stuffing out of my two daughters and wife. As I was gathering my notes to pack them back into my Bible, I looked up. Nobody was moving. Didn't they hear my amen? All good church people know that's code for "Wake up! It's time to go to the restaurant!"

I stood in front of the church waiting for someone to move. Silence had hijacked the sanctuary and had us all as its willing hostages.

I'll just stand here while they just sit there.

I sensed a professional pressure to tell a joke or say something profound, but I brushed off the temptation to perform and just stood. I looked out into the congregation and noticed the pylon lady, the lady who once stared through me, was now looking at me. Her manicured hands clenched the pew ahead of her as she stood up. Her body tilted forward, letting the pew carry her weight like a crutch. Before a word came out of her mouth tears came flowing out of her eyes. Everybody's attention was pointed in her direction, eagerly waiting to hear what a week's worth of just sitting there sounded like. Nobody but God knew what was going to happen next, and He wasn't telling, as least not then.

With her head hung down in shame she whispered, "Every day I live with guilt. I wake up with guilt. I go to work with guilt. I eat with guilt.

I go to sleep with guilt. Guilt in front of me, guilt behind me." She lifted her eyes. "I've been drowning in guilt for years, and I'm tired of treading water. Sometimes it feels like it would be easier to sink than swim." She kept standing but quit speaking.

I confess that at that point I didn't have a clue what to do. I knew there was a lot more inside her, that she was weighing the risks and rewards of telling the whole truth to the whole church. What if she divulges she's sleeping with the pastor? What if she admits to some heinous crime? What if she beats and abuses her children? I didn't know what caused her guilt; I wasn't sure if that was the right place and time for the truth. Yes, I know how that sounds crazy coming from a pastor, but I have heard way too many people tell the truth in church only to be kicked to the curb for doing so. Hers was a huge risk worth my internal debate and silence.

I was caught off-guard. I was scratching my head trying to recall any good verses I could slide her way on guilt. I made a living by saying words, but I couldn't stumble on a one that would have made her secret guilt vanish. Even if I had had an epiphany regarding guilt, I didn't know what had caused hers. A crime? A crisis?

One of the wisest decisions I made that week was to say nothing; I just stood and listened. We all sat there wondering if we really wanted to hear what was coming next.

Grabbing all the courage she could find, she said, "My teenage son committed suicide a few years ago. It's all my fault. I'm a terrible, terrible mom. I noticed his music and mood changed, but I thought that was just a teenager being a teenager. I should have seen the signs; I should have said or done something different. How could a good mom be blind to the darkness that surrounded her own son? Every day I replay and relive the past, hoping for a different ending, but it always ends the same—he's gone. For years guilt has choked the meaning of life out of me. I can't remember the last time I laughed. Even if I could laugh I would feel guilty about feeling good. I wish I could make a deal with God, my life for my son's. I know as a Christian I'm not supposed to think that way, but I do, and that piles more guilt on me. I'm getting tired of dog paddling, trying to stay above water anymore. This was going to be my last week treading water. A friend told me about these church services, and I felt I had nothing to lose by showing up. All week I just sat here thinking this was a waste of time, God doesn't care about my pain. I felt like I deserved the stiff verdict of guilt and pain for being such an awful mom."

Right at that point I was feeling guilty for opening a wound with my sermon I was not prepared to heal. I wish I'd said amen after all the good stuff God had been doing minutes earlier. There I was, pondering going home and hugging my wife and daughters, and she had been pondering taking her life. The whole congregation was eavesdropping on this broken woman's past and her public confession.

When we all thought she had gone down for the last time, when we thought maybe this was just too big and broken for even God to fix, she lifted her head up toward heaven and said, "Grace."

Wait a minute! She just said "grace." That doesn't sound like a person giving up.

She said, "For years I have been drowning in guilt and shame. I was ready to take my life because my son took his. I felt I lost my purpose in life when I lost my son. What can God possibly do with someone as broken as me? I don't remember much of anything you preached on this week accept one sentence. Earlier tonight you said, 'When we can't find grace, grace will find us.' Preacher, grace found me tonight. I know this is going to sound like I'm crazy, but when you said that sentence it was like a tidal wave of grace swept over me, washing all my guilt and shame away. Now all I can see is His grace and mercy."

I responded, "No, that doesn't sound crazy. That sounds like God."

"I feel like God loves me and He's not punishing me, so why I should punish myself? I guess if God loves me, then He may still have a purpose for my life, right?"

I assured her, "God seldom wastes our pain of the past. He has this awkward way of using the pain of our past to help heal others who are still stuck in theirs."

I've sung "Amazing Grace" a ka-billion times, but that night I got to see what it really looks like outside the pages of an aging hymnal. God truly had covered for my cluelessness that night. I have never claimed to be the smartest pastor in the world, but, wow, had I missed that one! I was saying amen, but God was saying not yet. I was putting away my sermon notes; God's love was still writing them. I was thinking of my kids at home, but God was thinking of the kid she had lost.

I shook her hand as she was walking out of the church. She took a few steps toward the door, turned around, and smiled for the first time in a long time. You and I know nothing could bring back her son; we can't change the past no matter how hard we try. God's not into the "me for you" deals. Moses and Paul in the Bible tried that one, and though God appreciated their hearts, He didn't sign on the dotted line.

Here was a fifty-year-old woman who had lost her son and hope all in the same day. Here was a person who had traded in all her guilt for all His grace. Guilt for grace is a deal God is always willing to sign off on. It was amazing how when she couldn't find grace, grace found her, even when she just sat there.

30
Me Time

My phone was blowing up with more problems than I could fix. I was feeling like a very stressed-out pastor that day. I had couples in marriages who once had said, "I do" but were then saying, "I don't." I had children tragically dying before their parents. I had more bills than our bank account was going to cover. I had some people telling me I was the worst pastor they knew. During a day like that one I was starting to believe them.

I had not taken my days off, feeling the church would fall apart if I wasn't there. My mind was somewhere in between quitting ministry and four weeks in the Bahamas. After reviewing our finances, I realized neither choice was realistic. I decided to take a day off and do nothing for nobody but me. I promised God for the sake of my sanity to not help Him repair the world for one day. As my wife would put it, I needed some serious "me" time.

It was a great morning. I woke up and treated myself to a pork-overload breakfast (ham, bacon, and sausage with loads ketchup) and Coca-Cola. I went to the bookstore for a book to disappear into for a few hours. The temperature was in the upper seventies as I drove down near the river near our house. I rolled down the windows, soaking in the sun while watching freighters slowly drift down the river. I turned off my phone and my mind, two perfect ingredients for some quality "me" time. I could feel my stress slowly starting to fade away.

After a few hours of unwinding I heard a grinding noise outside my window, the sounds of an engine trying to start. I noticed an older woman trying to start her minivan. This happened for about five minutes until the battery finally threw in the towel.

She looked at me with those woman eyes that said, Now what?

I quickly turned my head the other way, reminding God and myself of my mandatory me time. I told myself God was on His own that day; it was my day off. I figured if He could turn water into wine He could start a goofy minivan. I went back and plunged my nose deeper into my spiritual book, pretending I hadn't witnessed the slow death of her battery. After several minutes of reading I glanced to my right; she was still staring at me with a helpless look on her face.

The more I tried not to think about her, the more I thought about her, and I began trying to justify myself. Hey, there are fifty cars around us! One of them can help. Besides, I don't have jumper cables as if thinking that would slay my guilty thoughts. Wrong! My guilt was getting louder and louder, demanding I do something. Okay. I'll turn back on my phone and call a tow truck. Looking over at her, I saw her on the phone; she'd beaten me to that punch, so the distraction to my me time was resolved, and I was free to go back to doing nothing. As the minutes slowly ticked by I noticed no tow truck had shown up to perform CPR on her dead battery. After much wrestling, guilt finally kicked me out of my truck.

"Can I help?"

"I think it's my battery, but I don't know how to jump a car."

I asked her if she had cables. She did. The whole resurrection of the dead battery swiped only six and a half minutes from my me time, but I was still mentally whining about it. Why do I have to do all God's dirty work on my day off?

She went way over the top, trying to pay me and praise me for my six-and-a-half-minute miracle. I told her it was fine, no big deal. She insisted I had no idea the difference I had made, which dumped only more guilt on me because of my delayed response to her dilemma. She was almost crying with gratitude for this simple task. Then she slammed her minivan in reverse and flew out of the parking lot like an Indy driver. Wow, she must be in a hurry!

I went back to my me time, dozing off, pretending to read my book. I told myself and God the rest of the day was mine to do nothing ...

A few weeks later I was preaching a sermon at church on "serving others." I poked fun at myself, using the battery situation to prove more of what not to do. They all had a good laugh at my expense, but each shared they too had had similar "me" time stories.

After the sermon, a woman came up to me and said, "Dennis, I have something I think you should read." I probed her for a bit more info, but she said, "I'll bring it to you next week."

The following week she indeed brought in a small article she had saved from the local paper a few weeks earlier, a story about a nurse who had parked by the river. The story told how she had received an emergency call about one of her patients, but when she tried to start her minivan the battery conked out. She said she hadn't known what to do. She told of this guy who had come to her and her patient's rescue by jumping her dead battery. He never left his name, and she tried to pay him, but he wouldn't take it. She just wanted to thank him for helping her that day.

As I read the article praising me for my Boy Scout good deed of the day, somehow I didn't feel so worthy of it. Someone's life could have been on the line that day. Someone could have died because of my delayed obedience. I would have never known it. It never would have read "due to some guy who didn't jump a dead battery" as the cause of death on the certificate.

When I read that article I was embarrassed. I do believe we all should take our days off. I believe God can do just fine without us running the world for a day or two. I believe me time is a very good thing, but it does not mean burying ourselves in books and putting on blinders, trying to make the world go away.

Picture yourself in a major crisis crying out to God, "Please help me or I'm not going to make it."

I'm sure glad God does not respond, "Oh, sorry dude, day off—me time, you know…"?

31

Ordinary

"**O**rdinary"—just hearing the word sparks more of a yawn than a roar. Seldom does anyone grow up bragging, "I want to be ordinary!" Most of my life I have labeled myself as an ordinary guy just a little south of a C student. I have no MVP trophies collecting dust over our mantle. The president has never called to solicit my views on the war, the economy, or health care reform. Steven Spielberg has never sought me to be in one of his blockbuster movies. I was not the valedictorian of my class; I can't even spell valedictorian without spell check. The Detroit Tigers have not drafted me to be their starting pitcher or even their batboy. I have lived my whole life in the yawn of ordinary.

There are times late at night when I unleash my mind to ponder what it would be like to find the cure for AIDS or cancer. What if it were me hitting a game-winning grand slam in the bottom of the ninth instead of a bloop pop-up to end the game? What if it were me donating millions of dollars to bring relief to Third World countries? I just want to do something, say something, and be something great! I wish I could do something to magically spike my life's grade to a respectable B. When I die I want the poor sap doing my funeral to have something of value to say about me without lying.

But most of my days are just a pile of average minutes that melt into average hours that add up to the grand total of an average day that washes all my what ifs away. Wake up, eat the same breakfast (chocolate donuts and Coke), get in the same car, go to the same job, come home to same house, and sleep in the same bed just to wake up and do it all over again.

For most of Jesus' adult life he was an ordinary carpenter. His business cards simply read Joseph & Son; no dream job by any stretch of the imagination. It was a job that made people notice more what you did than who you were. He lived an ordinary life for thirty years. He walked on no water. He opened no blind eyes. He preached no sermons. He healed no lepers. He transformed no box lunches into hillside buffets. He didn't raise the dead. He was just one of hundreds of Jewish carpenters of His day with calloused hands and a healthy appetite.

There are many names that spring to our minds at the mention of the name "Jesus," including Healer, Miracle Worker, Teacher, Son of God, Compassionate, and Holy, but "ordinary" is not one of them. To call Jesus ordinary would be like invoking lightning bolts from the heavens. But for dozens of years he was an ordinary carpenter who built chairs, tables, and tools. He would wake up, pound some nails, eat meals, go home to bed, then wake up to do it all over again. For all those years no one had any idea the man who had built their kitchen tables was God disguised in blue jeans. No one had any clue—even his own brothers and sisters didn't fully know whom they were rooming with. He never said, "Hey, look at me! I'm God!" Jesus was an ordinary man with an ordinary job living in an ordinary town, Nazareth, a place not mentioned in the Old Testament. Such lack of respect was likely due to the unpolished dialect, lack of culture, and moral laxity of its residents. When Jesus was interviewing His disciples, when finding out He was from Nazareth, someone piped up, "Nazareth! Can anything good come from there?"

But what a difference a day makes! After thirty years, God uncovered the Carpenter as his One and only Son. Let's just say people yawned more than cheered. You might imagine they would have applauded. "Wow, you're kidding! God in the flesh is living in our hometown of Nazareth? I knew there was something different about that kid. His humility seemed to always ring louder than his hammer. He always asked how the missus and I were doing. Once, when I had no money to pay for my furniture, he just looked at me, smiled, and winked, "This one's on me."

But that's not the way the story goes. In fact, when Jesus returned home with a toolbox full of miracles with their names on it, the people said, "Thanks but no thanks." Their exact words were, "Isn't this the carpenter's son? Isn't his mother's name Mary, and aren't his brothers James, Joseph, Simon, and Judas? Aren't all his sisters with us?" (Matthew 13:55–56). They still saw him as an ordinary man, a carpenter, just Joe's kid, the guy who built on my addition, the guy who fixed my roof, but surely not the Son of God. "Do you think we are fools? Why would God send the Messiah, the King of kings, the Great I Am, to live in our hick town?" Matthew almost apologizes for this anticlimactic story: "And he did not do many miracles there because of their lack of faith."

How many times when Jesus was growing up did he overhear ordinary people praying ordinary prayers? How many times did Jesus walk by a blind man wanting to heal him but knowing it was not his time? How many times did Jesus walk by a leper, reaching out to heal him but pulling back his hand, knowing it was not his time? How many times did he hear a women wailing over the loss of her baby and want to bring them both back to life but knew it was not His time? I imagine many times Jesus tilted His head toward the heavens, silently pleading for permission to trade his mallets for miracles, yet for some sovereign reason God repeatedly said, Not yet.

After living thirty years doing the nine-to-five gig, the Son finally heard His Father whisper, It's time. Jesus couldn't believe he could start revealing what He had been forced to conceal for thirty years. So Jesus, leaping for joy, began to leak it to the press. "I am the One you have been waiting for! What can I do for you? It's time!" You would assume there would have been a line from Nazareth to the North Pole with people saying, "Heal me." "No! Heal me! I was here first!" "Stop taking cuts!" The story had the powerful potential to change this ordinary town into a sort of Disneyland, where dreams come true. Unfortunately, the tale stalls out a few sentences before they lived happily ever after. They saw Jesus as too ordinary, too much like them to help them.

It's easy to scratch our heads with confusion over those knuckleheads in Nazareth, but in some ways we are just like them. I've lost count of how many times in my ordinary life God has tried to bust in to save the day only to have me say, "No thanks, it's not Sunday at 11 a.m.," the only time many people feel God can work.

I was once standing in line at the grocery store, watching what seemed to be a single mom juggling her infant and purse like a circus clown as she sifted for extra cash. I felt God asking me to pay for her groceries. I began to question this feeling and wanted to see a sign that it was truly God talking. I began mentally tabulating the cost of what she was buying: milk, $2.99; bread, $1.87; hamburger, $5.99 ... I calculated if we had enough in our account to cover this God request. The mom pulled out food stamps but still came up a bit short. Embarrassed, she asked the cashier to take this and that away. I rushed in and paid for the few items she had left behind. She was overwhelmed. "Wow! Why would you do that for me? Thank you, sir, thank you, sir!" I smiled with the sense that God was pleased with my impersonation of the Good Samaritan.

After paying for my bulging cart of groceries, I left the store feeling pretty darn good about myself. But as soon as my foot hit the parking-lot blacktop I felt like God whispered, You missed it.

I missed what? I did what you asked me to do!

I didn't ask you to pay for her this and that—I asked you to pay for everything."

Trying to fulfill God's request, I looked around the parking lot to give her outside what I should have given her inside. I had no idea what God would have done for either one of us if I had acted more like a pastor than an accountant. At the time it seemed like such an unspiritual, ordinary moment.

Too often God wants to be included in our ordinary lives but we miss it. The apostle Paul wrote it well: "So here's what I want you to do, God helping you: Take your everyday, ordinary life—your sleeping, eating, going-to-work and walking-around life—and place it before God as an offering (Romans 12:1, The Message). Paul is not asking us to chisel our lives up into nice, even squares of secular and spiritual areas. Paul is giving us a blueprint for how we ordinary people can do extraordinary things if we only take Him grocery shopping.

I seem to use my average life as an excuse to not attempt anything great. When God asks me to do something over my head, I mentally scan my spiritual transcripts and say, Hey God, what about them? They got A's in "Love Your Enemies." God, that guy has a degree in "Thees and Thous," so pick him. God, why are You asking me to write a book when I struggle to write a sentence? God, why don't You pick someone more qualified?"

God loves to do amazing things through ordinary people in ordinary places. God is not looking for just the brightest or the best; He is looking for people like you and me, factory workers, schoolteachers, athletes, waitresses, coaches, students, and homemakers. When God chose twelve men to play on His team He didn't draft professional preachers, theologians, and priests; instead, He chose fishermen, tax collectors, laborers—common, ordinary folks just like us.

I wish I had known back then what I know today; God just flat-out loves me, and there is nothing I can do about it. God loves you, and there's nothing you can do about it. God doesn't love us because we cure AIDS, hit home runs, give loot to the poor, or have a mantle full of dusty trophies. He loves us because He likes hanging out with us and wants us to hang out with Him. He loves when we take Him to soccer games. He loves when we take Him to school. He loves when we take Him to work. He loves it when we take Him grocery shopping. I think I could even prove He loves it when we take Him to church. God never intended His love to be corralled into four walls, two hours, and six songs.

Two thousand years may separate us in time but surely not in how ordinary people miss it. Jesus came home ready to flip His old stomping ground into holy ground, and they missed it! Too often we look for God in the supernatural and miss Him in the supermarket.

We will always miss it when we let the facts take cuts on our faith. I knew God had asked me to buy that lady her groceries, but I let the price of milk get in the way of a mom's miracle. They called Him Healer, Miracle Worker, Teacher, Son of God, Compassionate, and Holy; but first they called him … dare I say it? … ordinary.

Whew. No lighting!

32
Sixth-Grade Sissies

The rumors had been swirling like bees around watermelon since third grade about sixth grade. I was warned if you didn't fit in, those eighth graders, the size of Amazon gorillas, would cram you in a locker like a math book. If that wasn't bad enough, the buzz had it that if you didn't comply with the junior high bullies, you could have parts of your anatomy flushed down the toilet. One kid told me an eighth grader had walked up and belted him for just being a sixth grader. All these things were tempting me to fail fifth grade till I was twenty-five or weighed in at 232 pounds.

After I accidently passed elementary school, my parents forced me to attend Bulliesville, otherwise known as junior high. I grew up in a Christian home but was never a real fan of prayer. Until then. I was begging Jesus to save me from the Devil and his eighth-grade employees. I was several pounds overweight and had not caught up with my cool yet. (My daughters would say I still have not caught up.) I had zits the size of Mt. Everest decorating my face like a pepperoni pizza. I was cursed with hair that would not lay flat even with a barrel of mousse. My nose was flat, and my ears were small. When I looked in the mirror all I saw was a big bull's-eye for bullies.

When I got into sixth grade, I found out most of the rumors were slightly exaggerated. Until the last week of school. I was walking down the hall not paying attention and bumped into one of the eighth-grade apes dragging his knuckles.

I knew it was not going to be a good day. I pretended to act like it was his fault and kept walking. He called me out in front of a packed hall of kids who were just itching for one more fight before summer break. My walk turned into a sprint.

He beat his chest and yelled, "Tomorrow I'm going to kick your butt." I tried to convince him that I was allergic to pain and that I fainted at the sight of blood, but that only motivated him more. I tried to reason by explaining that I was a pudgy sixth grader, and, well, he looked thirty years old and twelve feet tall, and he had a full beard—not fair. He repeated, "Tomorrow after school, me and you."

I went home and quizzed my parents if we had Blue Cross and Blue Shield.

"Why, Dennis?"

"Weeeeeeeeell, there's this bully at school who wants to fight me tomorrow, and he's the size of a Winnebago."

I prayed my dad was going to take pity on his sixth-grade sissy and give me permission to skip school. For the rest of junior high. That prayer, like so many others, went unanswered. My dad had grown up in a much tougher neighborhood than ours, or at least that's what I heard over and over. He bragged about some playground scrape he'd won two hundred years before. He gave me permission to stand up to this bully attached to some life lesson about not running away from our battles. My dad's macho-man spirit was getting excited about his boy not backing down from a fight.

He reviewed a few boxing tips with me. "Always cover your face."

"Really, Dad? That's the first tip you give me? Cover my face? I'm not feeling real good about my chances with the hulk in this junior high death match."

I went to school the next day having let my dad know I was strongly, very strongly, opposed to violence in public schools. I whined, "If you love me, how can you throw me to the lion?"

He seemed to put his Christian compassion on hold. "You have to learn how to stand up for yourself someday. Might as well be today."

I went the whole day ducking and weaving my way through the halls trying to avoid the sight of the Neanderthal. It was the last hour of the day, and I had this wonderful, consoling thought that maybe he'd caught yellow fever and was in the hospital or something.

Just when I thought it safe to exhale, I spotted him, and he spotted me. He stomped toward me, ready to make good on his threat.

People started yelling out, "Fight! Fight! Fight!"

I squealed out, "No, No, No! There's no fight! You can all go home now."

The students circled us, forming a human boxing ring.

Well, I had no place to run and no place to hide. I saw this movie once where the dude pretended to be insane and his opponent backed down. I begin to act like I was crazy, yelling out stuff that I'd heard on "Big Time Wrestling."

I threatened him terribly. "You wanna piece of me? I may be only a sixth grader, but I'm in it to win it." I flexed my flabby arms waving like thin flags in the wind. I was desperate, scared, and praying God could spare a few of his burly angels for a few minutes.

Then to my surprise he started to back down. I couldn't believe it! Hallelujah! It was a miracle! All this crazy stuff was paying off! I should have been happy he was backing down, but noooooo, I kept my big mouth moving. I continued to shoot out threats like I was the king of the jungle, at least junior high. I'd thought this guy could have pummeled me into the marble floors, but he was unclenching his fists! I heard laughter erupting all around me. Wait—there's no giggling in a death match.

For some reason I spun my head around. Standing behind me was the only eighth-grade friend I had. He had been perched behind me the whole time with his right fist clenched and nodding his head back and forth, letting the bully know, You touch him, I touch you. I was very excited that no blood had been spilled, particularly mine.

I asked my eighth-grade guardian angel why he had done it, why he had stood up for me.

He said, "You're my friend. I got your back even if you are a sixth grader."

I felt special that day, like someone had been looking out for me. When I got home, my dad asked for all the juicy details of the brawl in the hall.

"He backed down …"

"Yeah, I knew that would happen when you stood up for yourself."

I went to bed that night thanking my friend and God for sticking up for a sixth-grade sissy.

I'm writing this story on the Saturday wedged between Good Friday and Easter. Many Fridays ago Jesus stood up to the world's biggest bully, Satan. Jesus took a whuppin' that should have been mine and yours. He was getting the stuffing beaten out of him while the world stood around yelling, "Fight! Fight!" His blood was splattered all over the floor. No eighth grader ran to his rescue. No one said, "I got your back." He fought a fight we had no chance of winning, and He won. But his victory cost him His life.

I'm not in sixth grade anymore, but that evil bully still threatens me, pushes me around, and tells me how he's going to kick my butt. He tells me I'm worthless and I have no purpose in life. He tells me God's mad at me for some stupid thing I did in my past. He tells me, "You're not worth dying for."

Today I'm glad I remembered one day way back in junior high. It helped me understand the true meaning of Easter. I've preached Easter sermons so many times that if I'm not careful it will lose its true meaning. Easter is about someone standing up to the devilish threats that are pitched our way daily. Easter is about us doing the crime and Jesus doing the time. Easter is about Jesus rushing into our junior high halls and going toe-to-toe with bullies too big for us to battle. Most of all, Easter is about Jesus dying for sixth-grade sissies, and yes, even the eighth-grade bullies who beat them up.

33

Almost Too Busy to Pray

It was late when the phone rang. It was that time of night when you know it's not a salesperson. I almost didn't answer it; I had a hunch it was bad. When I picked up the phone, it took only a few seconds for the screams to confirm my hunch. It was a frantic woman from the church yelling, "It's over, it's all over."

"What's over?

"I'm' not going to take it anymore it's over. I'm going to shoot myself tonight."

Trying to pretend I was awake, I pleaded with her. "No, no—don't do that. Just talk with me for a few minutes."

I quickly began to snoop around for any clue as to what had led her finger to the phone and the trigger. I didn't have to snoop too far. She unloaded about a broken marriage that was a million miles away from the original "I do." She told me she'd caught her husband with another woman. Not just any woman, but one of her best friends.

"I hate him for doing this to me and the kids. The way I see it, I have three choices right now: one, shoot him; two, shoot her; or three, shoot myself. I'm choosing number three. That will show him! Let him deal with the guilt of my death for the rest of his life. Serves him right!"

I tried to tell her about the guilt her kids would be forced to deal with for the rest of their lives. I told her with suicide you can't change your mind tomorrow. She was so broken she couldn't see beyond the barrel of her gun. I quickly scampered for something clever to make sense in this chaos.

I interrupted her game of Russian roulette by asking, "What about your future?"

She gave a rehearsed line, something like, "I have no future without my husband. I can't believe he did this to me."

I asked her if I could come over just to talk, and that's when she hung up the phone. I was freaking out. What do I do? Do I call the police? Do I go over there? What if she turns the gun on me, or worse, is already dead? My fear had almost paralyzed me into doing nothing.

I told my wife and kids I loved them just in case something went terribly wrong in the next few minutes. My wife prayed with me, and I was off to do whatever I could.

When I got to the house, I knocked and knocked with no response. I told God, See? I tried, oh well. As I started to walk away, He reminded me to check if the door was open. Rats, He's right. I twisted the handle, slowly pushing open the door, not knowing what was behind it.

The house was very dark except for a dim light in the kitchen. I kept calling her name with each step I took. When I got to the kitchen, she was sitting on the floor, propped up against the wooden cabinets. Her black mascara was smeared all over her face. One hand was raking through her matted black hair, and the other was lying limp on the floor. She was surrounded by three things you never want to see in the same room together: a loaded gun, a suicide note, and an empty fifth of whiskey. She just kept staring at me and the gun like we were both her only hope.

She looked at me and slurred her words. "It's over. It's all over. I can't do this anymore. It's hopeless. He's gone. If I don't kill myself, I'll kill them."

I had thousands of hours of college classes under my belt but nothing on my tongue; I didn't know what to say. I had had many suicide calls, but I did most of the counseling over the phone. I was so scared to say the wrong thing that I said nothing. I was helplessly standing over her, watching her having a nervous breakdown. I wanted to say something, but nothing sounded good enough. I was silently begging God, Say something … anything … to one of us.

I wanted to give her a stack of verses on what the Bible says about suicide, but I just stood there. All I could think was that I didn't want either one of us to die, but I didn't know how to keep that from happening. I reminded God this was not a good place or time to put heaven on mute.

Then out of nowhere I felt God asked me to tell her about my day.

Are you crazy, God? Who cares what I did today? Who cares where I ate at? Who cares what my wife and I talked about at breakfast? No offense, God, but if I don't say something pretty quick we are both going to have a huge mess on our hands. Is that it, God? Just tell this lady with a gun an inch away from her fingers and a funeral about my day? Is that the best you got?

God just kept saying, Tell her about your day.

Then pow! Right in the kisser it hit me, and I begin to laugh.

She spoke up. "How can you stand there and laugh when I'm ready to blow my brains out?"

I told her, "Let me tell you about my day."

She said she didn't care what I had done that day.

"I know," I replied, "That's what I thought a few minutes ago too, but let me finish. Earlier this afternoon I was working at the church and felt like God asked me to go out and pray over the community. It was a hectic day, and I told God I was way too busy to pray. I had a sermon to prepare, meetings to attend, and I hadn't worked out. After a short tantrum of whining I gave in and started walking the streets. I walked all over this city, looking for whatever it was God wanted me to find. Either God was not speaking, or I was deaf, but either way I heard nothing. As I was walking, all I could think about was all the stuff I could be getting done for the church if I was in my office."

She was looking at me as if I'd lost my mind.

"But wait! This is where the story gets good." I told her that just when I was ready to quit and go back to my busy pastor thing, God spoke. "He told me to come by your house and pray for you."

"What the hell are you talking about?"

"I know. It sounds crazy, but earlier today I was standing next to your house with my hands pressed on your vinyl siding, praying for you and your family. To be truthful, I felt embarrassed as cars drove by with people probably wondering who that guy was, touching your house and talking to himself with no one around."

She leaned into the conversation with a ray of hope, asking, "Well, what did God say?"

"Now that I think about it, I don't remember what He said."

"So then what's the point of your religious fairy tale?"

"The point is ... I remember what I said to God. I asked Him to watch over and protect you."

"Well, I guess God didn't hear your little prayer. Can't you see I'm sitting here with an empty bottle, a full gun, and a note ready to end it all?"

"You're right," I answered. "You can end it. You can blow off everything I said as a fable or coincidence. You can put the gun to your head and pull the trigger, your choice. Listen, I don't walk on water, heal the blind, or have a beard like Jesus, and I definitely am not perfect, but I am here. You are alive. Say what you will about God, but He sent me here to let you know there is hope. I know you feel betrayed by your husband, but God is not your husband. He will not run when things get difficult and dark. He wants you to know that He knew at one o'clock in afternoon what you were going to do at one in the morning. Don't you get it? God loves you so much; He interrupted my busy pastor gig to pray for you. Sadly, I almost missed it, thinking I was too busy to pray, but I did pray for you and for your protection. You aren't even a member. I didn't call you tonight, you called me. What are the chances that the person to whom you made what you thought was your last call had been standing here hours ago praying for you? That seems to me to be a miracle. That is the love of God alerting you it's not over. You do have a future."

I sat on the floor with her, giving no rah-rah speeches or sermons. I simply extended my hand; she grabbed the gun and placed it in my hand and started to cry. We both exhaled, and I stayed long enough to talk her sober. She thanked me for saving her life, but we both knew God had lent us a few angels that night.

I went home and slipped into bed, interrogating myself. What would have happened if I'd been too busy to pray? What would have happened to that lady if I'd blown off God's nudge due to being busy with "pastor" stuff? Would she still be alive? I tried to shake off the notions. No, God would not have put the fate of another person in the hands of my undernourished prayer life. That possibility is a scary thought for me and others.

Often I justify my lack of prayer to God by all the things I am doing for God. Sometimes I get so busy doing God stuff that I miss God Himself. I cram my days with meetings about God, read books about God, prepare sermons about God, and still miss God. I bet there are days I'm so busy God Himself could walk into my office asking to see the pastor and I'd ask, "Do you have an appointment?" Sometimes I think, Oh, God will do what God will do with or without my modest prayers. But what if God doesn't move unless we pray?

Thankfully that night I didn't have to figure that out. She had put down the bottle and the gun that night. Life was not a bed of roses for her from that day on; there were many more calls, tears, and prayers, but she's alive.

I don't know why every day two to three thousand people pull the trigger, killing themselves. For every one who does succeed, twenty others try but fail. Every thirty seconds a life is taken and a funeral is planned. As you are reading this, thousands of men, women, and teens are buying guns, drinking fifths, and writing notes, all duped by the timeless lie, There's no hope. It's over. Some will pull out their phones and make one last call, hoping someone, anyone, will talk them out of what the Devil had talked them into.

My schedule is pregnant with good things to do for God each day. I can get so busy I forget to pray. But on that day God had twisted my arm and put me in a full nelson until I gave up and prayed for that gal. I'm so glad I did. And so is she.

34

One Red Minivan and Three Drunks

I was very comfortable buried under one sheet, two blankets, and an overstuffed off-white comforter the size of Texas. It was smack-dab in the middle of a frigid Michigan winter, the only kind we get. Our thermostat was programmed to a satisfying seventy-three degrees. I was only a few blinks away from dreamland.

Then I heard what I thought was God asking me to get up and pray. I rolled over, ignoring the voice. That can't be God. It's bedtime, and I already prayed earlier. I did my best to fall asleep, yet God kept poking my conscience to pray. So I groggily tossed up a few prayers for my family, friends, and the church and substituted a yawn for an amen. I rolled over knowing I had fulfilled my late-night duties to the God who obviously never slept.

Sadly, my twenty-second prayers didn't drown out God's repeated voice asking me to pray. I informed God I had prayed.

No. I want you to drive downtown and pray.

What? You're kidding! That means I'll have to get out of bed, put on warm clothes, boots, scrape all the snow off our red minivan ... Plus, who am I praying for, and where do I go downtown?

I gently tapped my wife, trying to wake her up to let her know I was leaving. She rolled over, made the sound of a grizzly, and went back to sleep.

I flipped off the covers, put on some sweats, and jumped in the minivan. As I waited for it and me to warm up, I ask God once again, Where do you want me to pray and for whom? This is crazy!

Once again He said, Just drive and pray.

I stubbornly obeyed and started to drive around and pray as instructed. I went to our local churches and prayed for pastors and their people. I drove by restaurants and prayed for the waitresses and their families. I drove by the hospital and prayed for the sick. I drove down Main Street and prayed for all the businesses. I didn't have a clue what the heck I was doing. This seemed like such a foolish thing to do. Everyone's in bed but me. It was past 1 a.m., and I was half-asleep as I slushed around in unplowed roads, looking for something, anything, to satisfy God's vague request.

I was a few minutes from calling it quits and filling the vacancy under the covers again. I halfheartedly repented for not cracking the code of the where and the who of this spiritual goose chase. I was on my way home when I looked to my left and saw a parking lot full of cars. What's going on at 2 a.m.? I noticed it was one of our community's favorite watering holes. I decided to make it my last stop of the night. I drove through the parking lot, looking for an open spot to squeeze our red minivan into. After a few minutes of idling around the lot, I found a spot in the middle of a herd of snow-covered cars.

At 2 a.m. my prayers are generally not that spiritual and not that long, but I prayed each person would make it home safely. I prayed God would let them all know they were loved. After a few minutes of praying I seemed to get my second wind. I raised my voice and started shoveling a pile of fancy church words into my prayer. I must say I was pretty impressed with my prayers, at least as impressed as you can be at 2 a.m. in a snowstorm.

After impressing all heaven with perfumed prayers I heard a noise. I'm by myself. Oh no! I looked in my rearview mirror and saw the door magically open. I was freaking out. Maybe I'm still in bed and this is just some wild dream. Maybe it's a crazed serial killer who hates red minivans. I twisted my head to see what this ghostly commotion was about when two extremely loud girls and one quiet guy started to load themselves into my red minivan as if it were a taxi. I had been on a ton of "prayer drives" but this was a first. With one whiff I could tell they had tipped back way more than a few Diet Cokes.

The drunken trio started babbling something about something that made no sense, at least to me. They were laughing and singing a karaoke version of a Springsteen song. After the free backseat concert I asked them their names. The girls said their names and enlightened me that the guy with them was German.

"What?"

"Yeah, he's a German foreign-exchange student."

He chimed in, "Yah, I'm German."

The girls giggled. "We were showing him a good time, and we're ready to go." They slurred out, "Let go."

160

"Go where?" I played the role of the cabby, "Okay, where would you like to go?" They didn't respond, so I asked them to buckle up and shut the door.

I began to interrogate God. What am I going to do with three drunks at 2 a.m.? God, this is not what I expected. I did not get a clear answer, so I started driving around in the snow, waiting for them or God to tell me where we were going.

As they bounced around in the backseat, they asked me, "Hey, isn't this fun?"

"Oh yeah, this is fun. Couldn't think of anything better to do at 2 a.m."

As I was aimlessly driving around, a light turned yellow, and I slid halfway into the intersection before my van stopped.

As we sat at the red light, God decided to speak. Dennis, tell them how much I love them.

I chuckled at God's request. God, they are, well, ah, toasted, blitzed, smashed, tipsy, hammered, and plain ol' drunk. They can barely understand each other let alone You or me. But due to a lack of sleep and a great desire to go home, I agreed to pacify Him. Sitting in the middle of the intersection, I passed on the message. "Hey guys, I just want you to know how much God loves you." I probably could have added a bit more passion and zing to the message, but I simply passed it on.

They put their concert on mute and said nothing; they sat there buckled and bewildered. God, I told you they're drunk. This is exactly the way I thought this was going to go down.

Then one of them burped, "Wow! How cool is that? God loves drunks!"

I must admit it sounded a lot different when the German dude said it versus when I prayed it, but yes, God loves drunks.

I added, "You may not remember that tomorrow morning or the next. It might take twenty years, but someday you will know God loved you so much He shoved me out of bed to get you home safely tonight." I was just about to launch out into a sermon on our response to God's love when God put the brakes on my now early morning lecture.

Dennis, I told you to tell them I love them, not to preach a sermon.

I know, God, but I got them roped in the back like steers with no place to go. This is the perfect opportunity.

Whatever you say beyond "God loves you" I'm not endorsing.

The German guy interrupted my potential sermon. "Hey, the light is green. That means go, right?"

I laughed and said, "Thanks." I spun my tires in the direction of our next stop.

A few miles down the road one gal said, "We're here."

I pulled over. They unbuckled and exited the van, shouting a quick thanks with a smirk like they had just stiffed the taxi driver.

As I drove away I asked God, What was that all about tonight?

Dennis, you prayed all the right words tonight but had no heart in them. You were at the right spot for all the wrong reasons. You were just trying to fulfill your obligation to get Me off your back so you could go back to bed.

He must have been able to read minds, because that was actually what I had been thinking.

I went home, crawled under my one sheet, two blankets, and huge comforter. God, you did something really cool for three people who probably will never, ever thank you for it. Yes, that's true, they may not thank You, but three, no, four people will all go to bed tonight knowing I love drunks. But God? Why did you send me to them?

Because you have a red minivan and I don't.

35

Lunch

It was a beautiful, sunshiny day in Nashville, and the sun was splashing its rays everywhere. The temperature was in the upper eighties, and for a Michigander in May it was heaven. I was attending one of those "Learn How to Preach Better" seminars. Our morning speaker had just challenged all of us to be more attentive to the poor. He cited that around 3 billion people in the world work for approximately two dollars a day and one million work for one dollar a day. He shared that by the end of the day, and every day, over twenty thousand people would die due to starvation. By the time he ran out of wind he had most of us feeling guilty as well as grateful.

He challenged our faith with his facts to stop talking about poverty and start doing something about it. The pews full of us professional pontificators cheered in unison. Even a few stray amens and hallelujahs echoed throughout the auditorium. We gifted the speaker with a passionate standing ovation. After a benediction prayer we shooed off to lunch.

I had no lunch plans except to soak up an hour and a half of rented sun and to walk around the city. There were thousands of hungry preachers all sprinting to their favorite food joints. I got behind a convoy of pumped-up pastors trying to digest the homiletic all-you-can-eat buffet being served. I overheard some of the pastors commenting on what nuggets they were going to steal to feed their own flocks the following Sunday.

As I peeked ahead, I saw a head-on collision about to take place with our sermon we had just inhaled and real life. Outside a crowded restaurant stood a homeless man propped up against a light pole. He was partially dressed in a worn-out pair of beltless blue jeans and no shirt. In one hand he had half a dozen returnable cans in a plastic bag while his other hand was empty, stretched out, waiting to be filled. His messy hair draped over his sunburned, bony shoulders. The stories of his life faded into tattoos on his sun-dried skin. You could sense his body and mind were not at the same address. He was asking for anything from anyone.

Without turning his head, the leader of our pastoral parade moved to the left, just out of touching distance of the man. The others in the flock followed as though they were playing an unconscious game of follow-the-leader. How is this happening? These people just minutes ago heard what I heard and are now seeing what I see, and yet they are rushing past him to wait in line for lunch. What happened to the standing ovation, the amen corner, the thundering applause? What happened to all us pastors chirping "amen" and "hallelujah"?

What had happened? Twenty minutes earlier hunger had been halfway around the world. Twenty minutes earlier it had been words on a page and a stage. Twenty minutes earlier it had been a library of facts without faces. But now detouring around a human billboard of the sermon we had just praised.

It's always easier to give ethical and spiritual commentary on what others should do versus looking in the mirror. All I have to do is look in the rearview mirror of my life to see the miles of helpless people I've left stranded on the side of the road with their hands out.

To protect our hearts from being punctured by guilt, we have a catalog of questions: Hey, why don't they just get a job? Don't they have any family who can help? What if they have a gun? If he has enough loot to buy cigarettes and booze, why can't he spend it on food? What if they buy drugs with my money? (God would not be happy with me spending His holy cash on crack). Why don't they just go to soup kitchen right down the street? If I give to one, I'll have to give to all. If he would just accept Jesus, everything would be alright.

It's odd that we will ask ourselves a dozen questions about giving five bucks to a stranger but not ask any questions about buying a twenty-five-hundred-dollar flat screen. Okay, maybe one: is it on sale?

All these questions led me to more questions. Why are they sleeping on the streets and me on a Serta? Where and when did their trains fall off the tracks? Does God love me more than them? I do believe there is a price to pay for sin, but why does their sin hurl them to the streets and my sin chase me to an altar? Why are we standing inches apart yet the Grand Canyon seems to separate our lives?

My questions were directed not at the preachers who walked by an empty stomach only to fill their own but at myself. What should I do? Do I walk by, following the sheep? Do I act like he's invisible? Do I just smile at him as though my silence will fill his growling, empty stomach? Do I give him a tract and tell him the good news about Jesus and how He can change his life?

I don't always know what to do about poverty. I don't know how much to give or to whom to give. At times I give out of guilt, at times I give out of pity, at times I give because someone is watching.

I didn't help them all that day but I did help one. The man standing at the pole will not retire on my measly contribution, but he was able to eat that day. I guess the best we can do is do our part. Many times I have no clue why I give, but that day I gave out of love. Not just love for a stranger but love for God. I didn't give because I had to but because I wanted to. I didn't give all I had, but I did give some of what I had. In some very small way I feel I made a difference at lunchtime to one shirtless man in Nashville.

I walked twenty feet down the road and heard a lady ask, "Hey mister, you got any spare change?"

36
Hot Tubs

We were invited to tag along with some friends to Florida over Thanksgiving. They told us if we could find our own way down there they would pay for our lodging. To Michiganders this was a no-brainer, substituting snow for sun.

The place was one of those plush, fully furnished time shares. It was a wonderful week stuffed full of Disneyland, Gatorland, SeaWorld, and outlet malls. Just a stone's throw from our condo was a gorgeous pool surrounded by four heated hot tubs.

I planned a nice, relaxing day by the pool for the last day of our vacation. It had been a busy week, and I had probably spent more time with Mickey than with God. I got up very early, before my family, and snuck out to the pool to redeem some quality time with God.

It was a perfect Florida morning, with temperatures slowly climbing to the mid eighties. Just me, God, and an empty hot tub, the perfect trinity for relaxation. I slipped into my private bowl of bubbles and started soaking up the sun and thanking God for a great week. I thanked Him for my family and all the blessings He tosses our way daily.

After about twenty minutes of solitude and silence, I noticed an older woman walking toward my hot tub. Why is she coming toward my hot tub when she could have selected one of the other three, which were empty by the way? I reminded God I wanted just some peace and quiet time with Him. God, I squeezed you out of our vacation, and I'm sorry about that, but hey, I'm trying to make it up now. I knew that when she sat she was going to want to chat and would thereby interrupt my spiritual sabbatical. My prophetic intuition was proven true after about fifteen seconds.

"Nice morning isn't it?"

"Yep," I grumbled.

She didn't pick up on my "closed for conversation" signals. "Where do you live?"

"Michigan," I closed my eyes and tilted my head back, stretched out my feet, and tried to reconnect with God. I picked up my prayers at the place where I had been interrupted: Father, thank you for this and that. Basically I was thanking God for my good life. I had learned over the years He likes when we do that kind of thing.

After a few minutes of my prayers and her silence she continued. "So are you on vacation with your family?"

"Yep." I would like to defend my brevity by saying I'm normally a bit more conversational, but that day was one of those I days I wanted to be left alone. I didn't want to be Pastor Dennis, just Dennis, just for a few hours.

After some forced small talk I realized my time alone with God was sunk. Plus I started to feel some guilt floating my way due to my selfish silence. I asked her one simple question that opened a huge wound.

"Where do you live?"

I thought it was a nice, safe question. I didn't ask her age, shoe size, or weight, just where she lived; that had been one of the questions she had asked me.

She was very slow to answer. "Well, right now I live no place."

Wait … everybody has someplace to call home. Maybe the morning sun's getting to her.

"No. I asked you where you live."

In a soft voice she replied, "I used to live in Texas, but when the bad storms came charging through, I lost my house and everything in it."

"Well, where do you live now?"

"I have no place to live. Friends have given me a few vouchers for hotels to stay at for a couple months."

"Don't you have family or kids to stay with?"

Embarrassed, she shook her head, letting me know that was another story.

"What will you do when you run out of free hotels?"

She lowered her head confessing, "I don't know where I will go."

"Do you have a church?"

"No, kinda in between churches right now."

Her dilemma caught me off-guard. I assumed that if she was staying in this swanky joint she had to be pretty well off. I assumed everybody here was rich, except us, of course. I felt terrible I'd been such a jerk for Jesus. I listened to her pour out her hurt. When she finished, she said, "I'm not looking for a handout, just someone to listen."

Trying to stumble upon some, any, shred of dignity, I ask her name about thirty minutes too late.

"Sally," she kindly whispered.

"My name is Dennis." I let her know I was sorry for the hand she'd been dealt. I asked her if I could pray with her.

"Here? Right now? In the hot tub?"

"Yeah, if you would like."

"Yeah, sure, I guess." She bowed her head like she was in church. Because she didn't seem like a churchgoing lady, I tried not to use any religious words but to keep it simple.

"Dear God, help Sally find some friends and a place to stay and let her know how much You love her, amen."

When I looked up you would have thought I had given her a brand-new house. She was beaming as bright as the sun above us, confessing, "Wow, that was great!" She told me that a lot of people had given her a lot of advice but no one had prayed with her. She couldn't believe that you clould pray in a hot tub. She thought that was funny.

"Who would have thought I'd get a prayer coming to a hot tub this morning?"

Clearly not me, I thought.

"Well, I need to be going. It was nice meeting you, and thanks for the prayer."

As she left I laughed at myself, wondering what God thought of me. Here He had moved all heaven and earth, at least part of Florida, to get a preacher and a homeless woman to the same hot tub, but the pastor had been too busy praying to pray.

37
Special Table

I received a lunch invitation from a group of Christian students at a local college. They'd heard I'd just moved to town and wanted to get to know me. As I was starting a new church in a new town, I thought it would be a great way to meet a few people. I told them thanks for the invite and asked where and when. They told me to meet them the next day at noon in the college cafeteria.

After hanging up, I realized I should have gotten a few more details about how I would spot them in a crowd. I walked into the cafeteria full of youngsters and felt as old as Methuselah. I panned the room for a group of "Christian" students, and sure enough I spotted them huddled by the food line. I must admit they made it pretty easy to spot them. Most were sporting Christian T-shirts giving Jesus some much-needed free advertising. Walking their way they all waved at me like they were in training for a Fourth of July parade.

When I walked up and introduced myself, they said, "Praise the Lord! Hallelujah! Glad to meet you, pastor, and so glad to have you as part of the team."

What team? I thought I was coming for burgers, fries, and a Coke. They bumped me to the front of the line to honor me as if I were the pope without the outfit. They paid for my meal, which was nice. I must admit I felt pretty important leading the pack. After they picked up the tab, I wandered off to put dibs on a table for me and my new teammates when someone from the group said, "Oh no, we have our own table."

"You have what?"

"We have our own, special table in the middle of the cafeteria."

I didn't understand that, but being new to the team I agreed to play by their rules.

We sat at the middle table surrounded by, let's just say people not wearing Christian T-shirts. I muttered silent thanks for my food and began to do my best to make my burger disappear, but before I could take another bite, the captain said, "Let's pray out loud, thanking Jesus for our daily bread." He reverently bowed his head and prayed a prayer with more words than a Stephen King novel. He concluded his sermon with a loud amen, followed by our table echoing out amen, amen, amen, like we were playing a game of Simon says.

I thought the fifty amens were giving me permission to attack my by-then cold cheeseburger. Wrong! The captain of team proudly chuckled, saying, "Oh, we forgot one thing."

I could tell I was the only one at the table with no clue about what was coming next. They all giggled like they were in junior high, knowing they'd forgotten the most important part of lunch. The kid next to me dug into his navy-blue backpack and pulled out a piece of paper folded in half, which he placed in the middle of our table as if it were a centerpiece. It had two big, bold black words professionally printed on it: GOD SQUAD.

"What are you doing? Why are you putting that billboard on our table?" I asked.

He wasted no time with his comeback. "How will they know we're Christians if we don't have our sign? This is our way of letting the sinners know they can join us if they want to. Pretty cool idea, right?"

"But don't you think it would be a better idea to sit with other students instead of at our own, special table?" I asked. Let's just say they didn't have to take a vote to turn my suggestion down. Thinking out loud, I said, "Maybe we could try to have one lunch and leave the billboard in the bag and see how it goes?"

He had this puzzled look that asked, But how would they know we are Christians without our sign? He felt it would be too risky to the squad's faith to sit with the other people. "Dennis, this is why we sit in the middle, so they can all see us."

"How many people have joined the God Squad this semester or any semester?" They all looked at me like this could be my first and last God Squad free-meal deal. They agreed to keep doing what they were doing with or without results.

I normally don't feel embarrassed to talk about or for God. I'm not ashamed to let people know I'm a Christian, but at that moment I wanted to crawl inside my backpack. My small brain could not figure out why they were waiting for all the "sinners" to come to them. It's not that they were not nice, but they were nice just to people who sat at their special table. I finished my burger, frozen at that point, and was silently given permission to leave the squad.

The next day I went back to the cafeteria, and that time the God Squad had no "Praise the Lords" or "Hallelujahs," nor were they rushing me to the front of the line. Worst of all, no free meal. I snagged a seat at one of the not-special tables a biscuit toss from theirs. When I looked over at the God Squad, they were staring at me like I was Judas Iscariot's twin. This was the official sign that I had been excommunicated from the squad.

Each day they would cluster in the middle of the heathens and talk about God and how to save their campus. Each day they would drag out their sign and invite new Christians to a free lunch and free seat at their special table.

I don't like to admit it, but I got what they were trying to do. When I'd finally gotten saved after years of dancing with the devil I'd done the same thing. I remember telling people the good news about being saved. I thought they would be so excited and dance the hokeypokey with me, but I was wrong. They laughed and said, "Yeah, right." I was so hurt they didn't believe me that I changed; I did what the Squad was doing. I bought one of every Jesus T-shirt in stock at a Christian bookstore. I walked out thinking, Now they will know I'm a Christian.

Funny, quick story: one of the first times I wore one of my new T-shirts in public didn't go very well. I was playing basketball with all the people not invited to the special table. The game got a little rough. Okay, really rough. One hairy, sweating, gorilla wearing a pair of Jordans kept bullying me around. I'd had enough and got up in his face, ready to scrap. I was clinching my face and fists, ready to give or receive a beating, but either way this thug had picked on the wrong guy. Just when World War III was ready to break out, he looked down at my chest and asked, "Hey, what's your shirt say?"

Forgetting my faith fashion choice for the day, I looked down and saw my "Jesus Loves You" T-shirt staring up at me. I was so ticked for wearing that shirt that day I told him, "You're lucky I'm wearing my Christian T-shirt or I would have pummeled you."

He mocked me and my shirt. "Well, I'm glad at least Jesus loves me."

I, like the squad, had been duped into thinking somehow my shirt would save the world. The only thing that shirt saved that day was me from getting my butt kicked.

At that moment I felt compassion for the God Squad; looking at them that day, I was not mad; they were just doing what they had been taught. Someone in their spiritual upbringing had tutored them to believe the way to change the world is through shirts and signs. They were told not to get too close to sinners because their transgressions could somehow contaminate their Christianity. Someone had taught them not to let sinners' tables touch theirs. They gathered in huddles every day, calling plays, but never saying "Break."

When Jesus told the God Squad (the Pharisees) of his day that he had come for sinners, not the saved, the sick not the healthy, let's just say that was the last time he was invited to sit at their special table. No more free meals for you, Jesus.

Sometimes we get so caught up in the Christian club thing that we don't even talk to strangers anymore. Some of us are born in the church and will die in the church and spend our whole lives condemning the world from the safety of the church. If we're not careful we can rely too heavily on our shirts, signs, and special tables to change the world. I don't want to oversimplify the death of Jesus, but had the God Squad crucified Him because He'd sat at the wrong table with the wrong people?

One New Testament writer named John (1 John 3) was asked the same question I had asked several years earlier, "How can a person spot those Christians in crowd?" His answer was simple: "You will know them by their love." Can you imagine John answering the question with, "You will know them by their shirts, signs, and tables"? It doesn't have the same impact but would probably be much easier. We assume if they won't believe in God by the way we live, maybe they'll believe by the way we dress.

One of the biggest criticisms Jesus still receives is that he ate and drank with sinners. When was the last time you got criticized for hanging around the wrong people at the wrong table?

38

$24.57 Chocolate-Chip Cheesecake Muffins

I was a tad frustrated that morning. I felt like God was clearly asking me to write a book, but I didn't know on what subject. I was beginning to think maybe He had been holding out on me. So I sought out a muffin joint to gulp down a breakfast of champions: a Coke and a chocolate-chip cheesecake muffin (just saying that sounds holy). I sat there staring at a blank piece of paper, wishing it would somehow magically write itself.

Then I remembered a writers' conference I had just attended. I'd learned that every book should answer a question that the potential reader was asking, so I scribbled words to that effect at the top of my naked page. The waitress came by and asked if I needed anything. I'm not sure why, but I blurted out the question, "If God walked into this restaurant, what would you ask Him?"

She sheepishly put her hands over her mouth, muttering between her fingers, "Ah, um … I don't know. Wow! That's a good question."

I could see she was stumbling for what she thought I wanted to hear, so I told her to think about it and stop back before I left. She agreed and dismissed herself.

I peeked over my shoulder to see and hear her repeating the question to her fellow muffin makers. A choir of chattering responses broke out; I heard everything but understood nothing. I was three Cokes in, down to licking crumbs from my wrapper, but no answer. Then God sparked a spiritual idea:

Go and buy another muffin and they'll have to talk to you. Okay, maybe it was not God, but any thought that includes two chocolate-chip cheesecake muffins I'm all in.

As I went to pay for my extra ten pounds, I could tell she was ready to give her well-pondered response.

"Well?"

She gave me what one of the other workers' answer was.

"Good," I said, "But what's your answer?"

She said, "Will you save me? I want Him to save me and take me with Him." I was shocked. Her answer proved she had taken the question far more seriously than I had asked it.

My first instinct was to pull out my handy-dandy Bible and give her a guided tour through the New Testament. But I didn't. I just said, "Lisa, that's a great question to ask God." She put it in reverse and retreated to the kitchen, not knowing if it had been what I had wanted to hear.

Another waitress walked up and asked, "Are you the guy who asked the God question?"

"Yes, I'm working on a book."

She asked me to repeat the question. I did. "What would you ask God if He strolled into your muffin place?"

She said, "Look out the window. Look at all the cars and people going by. Look at all these muffins and workers. I just would ask Him, 'Why?'"

"Are you asking 'why' like what's the meaning of life?"

With hesitation she said, "Yes, why all this stuff? Is there any meaning to our lives, or is all just a big blob of nothing?"

I photocopied my first answer a second time. "That's a great question to ask God."

As I was walking out, I stopped and said good-bye to the first gal, Lisa. I didn't give her a parting swat with a six-pound, leather-bound King James Version; I just confided to her that twenty-five years earlier I'd asked God the same question, "Would you save me?" and He had. "I think it's His favorite question to answer." I mixed in three more words: "Jesus loves you."

With water squeezing out of her eyes, she said, "Wow, thanks, thank you."

I sensed she felt unworthy of His love and her answer. I walked out and got in my truck, wondering if somehow I'd blown it. Should I have led them through the sinner's prayer? Should I have left my business card? Should I have crammed a couple of tracts into their mitts?

I went to a bookstore about a stone's throw from the muffin mecca and grabbed some books that addressed their questions. Twenty-four dollars and fifty-seven cents later I personally delivered two individually wrapped books to the two gals. One book talked about how Jesus loves us, and the other was titled Why? I walked in and saw Lisa and began trying to share why I was dropping off two books to two strangers, but before I could she called the other waitress over, and they both opened their gifts at the same time. I was hoping I was not being pushy, but before that thought was able to build any momentum they both freaked out.

"Wow, Why is the exact title to the question I just asked," she said.

Lisa said, "Jesus loves me. That's what you just told me."

Their grins gave away that they felt they had just gotten early Christmas gifts from a six-foot-three, 211-pound elf (plus 10 extra muffin pounds). By then the muffin makers in the back had heard the ruckus and had taken front-row seats for this spontaneous book giveaway.

As I was leaving again, one of them asked, "What's your name?"

"Dennis."

"Thanks so much for coming in, Dennis."

"You're welcome." I smiled and walked out.

I didn't know if they would be saved by the end of that day. I didn't know if they would flock to the church around the corner. I didn't know if they would read the books I'd given them. But here is what I did know: two muffin-making ladies would be closer to God at the end of their shifts than they had been at the beginning.

Here's the deal. I could have driven to any diner or dive from Michigan to Memphis and heard the same two questions: Am I worth loving? Does God have a plan for me? You don't have to be an evangelist to know the answers; they are yes and yes and will always be yes and yes.

I have boxes of dusty questions I've asked God for which I have no answers. One question is, "What do You want me to write this goofy book about?" Though I did not come out with a title that day, I did come out with a lesson. I know what God loves more than $24.57 chocolate-chip cheesecake muffins: the people who make and serve them and also the people who eat them.

39
Switch

Most of my Christian life had been pretty good; on my life before that I take the fifth. I clearly lived with the haves more than the have nots. God was way better to me than I was to Him. I had a fantastic wife and two kids who made life worth living. I was not perfect, but I'd done a decent job of not chipping too many pieces off the Ten Commandments. I prayed, read the Bible, tithed, and went to church regularly. When I talked about God, I spoke with passion and conviction. If you had asked me about God, I would have given you the company line, "God is good all the time, all the time God is good." I loved God, and God loved me. It was a beautiful thing.

But a trip to Africa during which I saw suffering I still have not found words for caused a darkness that would not go away. I woke up and it was dark. I went to bed and it was dark. Every day was darker than the day before. I kept bumping into walls, looking for light switches. Darkness had crashed my Christian party and was refusing to leave.

I tried everything I knew to get the light to shine on me again. I dropped to the floor face first, plunging my nose into the carpet, begging God for relief … but nothing. I tried to serve the poor, giving all my stuff away … but nothing. I called in some spiritual supermen to anoint and pray over me, and each one promised a healing … but nothing. I tried to do tricks for God to see if He would have pity on me and lift the anvil of gloom from around my neck … but nothing.

I was running out of tricks when I remembered the Bible talking about the power of fasting. That's it; I'll go on a long fast. So I bartered with God.

I'll go on a forty-day fast, and you give my darkness the boot, then everything can get back to normal.

About halfway through my fast I was carrying food downstairs at the catering place I was working at part-time, and I almost passed out. I dropped the food but caught myself before tumbling to a pair of broken legs or worse. Up to that point all the fast had gotten me was a cranky attitude and an empty belly.

I was very irritated with God. I'd served him faithfully for years. I hadn't asked Him to make me rich or famous. I'd helped scores of people day and night. I'd pointed thousands to the switch but couldn't find it for myself.

God, why won't you talk to me? How can I share the Light with others if I can't see it myself? Did I blow it so bad that You won't show Your face to me? I bragged to the world of Your unconditional love, but today I'm feeling more left out than loved. I feel alone, annoyed, and in the dark, always in the dark.

My faith had never been forced to survive in such a murky place. I had not experienced a time when God's lips were sealed so long. I was trying to keep God off the hook, so I began to do what I always did in the dark, blame myself. I woke up each morning to interrogate my sins, forcing them to confess something I'd done wrong, but I found nothing but a few misdemeanors. I started to make up sins I might have unintentionally committed and then beg for forgiveness to appease God.

What have I done so badly to tick God off that he won't speak to me? I thought He was a loving Father. What kind of dad leaves his kids in the dark, bumping into walls, while he is standing comfortably next to the light switch? I've done everything the books, CDs, sermons, and preachers said to do ... and still nothing.

At that point my once-fun, Christian life consisted of waking up and lying on the couch with a blanket covering my body so God would not see me like that. I locked myself in dark rooms so my wife and kids wouldn't be bothered by my darkness. I hated my kids seeing me that way. I felt like a terrible dad, empty and useless. I was so ashamed of where I was but didn't know how to find the switch.

Some of my friends noticed the dark cloud hovering over my head and began to talk. Some spiritual snipers began to take a few cheap shots at me and my misery.

"Hey, Dennis! What's wrong? Why don't you just pray harder? That's what you told us to do ... Why don't you go on a fast? That's what you told us to do ... Why don't you go buy a book at the Christian bookstore? That's what you told us to do ... Kind of funny, isn't it Dennis? All the Jesus stuff you preached to us doesn't work for you now."

I was so broken and hurt I didn't know if I would have been better off smacking them or agreeing with them. In a very dysfunctional way I felt I deserved the bullets flying my way.

I thought maybe they were right; maybe I needed to get out of the preaching gig and go back to the factory I'd come from. I kept trying to convince my wife that it was over, that I'd lost God's light and love.

I know I told the whole world you could never lose His love, but I screwed even that up. What a joke how can a pastor who makes a living out of spreading God's love loses it. I feel like the biggest hypocrite on earth. Yep, it's time to quit! I don't know if that's God's voice or the Devil's, but today they sound exactly the same.

I didn't want to live and I didn't want to die—I just wanted the darkness to go away. I was yanking my family and church down every day I remained in the dark. I was no fun to be around anymore. I'd lost my laugh; it had been years since I'd smiled a real smile, not the fake ones I displayed on Sundays, and everybody knew it. All I did was cry all day.

Just before she died, my mom was so pound of me she'd bought me a gold cross necklace knowing she was not going to make the whole journey with me. I felt such a disappointment to her that I ripped the chain off and hid it in our bathroom cupboard. I took down a beautiful picture of Jesus hanging on a wall and put it in our shed to room with our lawnmower.

Some days I woke up and teamed up with the Devil, taunting, Some pastor you are! You can't even get out of bed or stop crying. Nobody's going to want to come to a church where the pastor is more messed up than the parishioners.

I didn't know what to do! This couldn't have been God's will for my life. I was feeling as useless as an ashtray in church. I didn't know how to make the dark go away. Then a thought, a voice, tiptoed into my head. Kill yourself. At first I rebuked it. But I teach against that! I teach there's always hope. But the more I fought the voice, the weaker I became. After weeks and weeks of being mobbed by the voice, I decided to give up.

Maybe my family's better off without me. Maybe the church is better off without me. Maybe God is better off without me. I'm feeling like such a burden to my wife, kids, church, and God. I began to justify waving the white flag. Well, my wife will get a better husband ... my kids will get a better dad ... my church will clearly get a better pastor, and God can be done with me.

I knew the voice wasn't God's, but it seemed like God wasn't in the talking mood. I drove to the cemetery a few blocks from my house and laid down next to a grave, screaming at the sky, There, God. You got me, you win, I quit. I can't keep on living, dying, in the dark. Please take me now so my family can get on with their lives. Please answer this one last prayer: give my wife a better husband and my kids a better dad when I'm gone. I know what the Bible says about suicide, but I can't keep fumbling around in the dark looking for the switch anymore.

After hours of nothing but the Devil's voice and God's silence I decided to try something different. I got back in my car and drove to a busy intersection.

If You won't do it, I'll do it myself!

I felt like such a failure and that this was my only way out. I had one foot on the brake and the other on the gas. I was waiting for an eighteen-wheeler to come my way. I looked to my left. Rolling down the street was my ticket to heaven or hell, but I didn't care. Just as I was going to pull out I heard a song on the radio by Creed: "Hold me close 'cause I'm six feet from the edge and thinking maybe six feet ain't so far down." A song that someone else had written about life's darkness. By the time the line was over the truck had roared past and I was still alive but didn't know why.

I yelled at God, Why am I alive but feel so dead?

Confused and numb I drove home thinking things could not get worse, but they did. I was in the middle of starting a ministry that was going to call on me to travel to other churches to speak about the power of prayer. Then I received a call on my voice mail reminding me about a booking I had taken over a year earlier to speak at a church on prayer for a week.

Really? I laughed. A church wants a guy to speak on the power of prayer? A guy who almost just took his life? They would have to be pretty desperate or dumb to want me and my baggage.

I know it was not the right thing to do, but I did it anyway: I decided to lie to the pastor by telling him I was deathly sick and would not able to preach at his revival meetings. My wife caught wind of the white lie, but I was sick!

"Dennis, God knew you'd be broken when you booked this church. God knew you'd be lost in the dark."

"Heidi, it's not fair to speak to a church about the power of prayer when I don't believe in that stuff anymore. How can a guy who feels he's lost God's love tell others how to find it?"

"Just be honest with the people and tell them where you are. Invite them into your darkness."

Yeah right, that's a good one! "Ladies and gentleman, tonight's sermon is an invitation into the worst period of my life, so come join me." Not going to work. People are paying me to preach on the power of prayer and not to be forced into a dark room without a switch.

I was mad at her not because she was wrong but because she was right. I decided to call the pastor and give him a way out if he wanted to take it.

"Hi, pastor, this is Dennis Cook."

"Oh, hi Dennis! We've been praying for our time with you."

"Yeah, that's what I want to talk to you about. Something happened, and I'm not doing too well right now."

"Dennis, are you sick? We can reschedule." There it was. My loophole, my way out. All I had to do was fib and ask for forgiveness after I hung up.

I paused. "I'm messed up really bad. I seem to have done something wrong that has caused darkness to have taken up permanent residence in my life. Please don't be mad at me for saying this, but I feel I have somehow lost God's love."

At that point I was waiting for fire and brimstone to come flaming through the phone from an angry pastor. But this gentle man said, "Dennis, God knew you would be in this dark place when we booked this."

I thought my wife had called him and warned him of my gloomy situation, but she still denies it.

"Dennis, you'll do fine."

I interrupted his kindness with my reality. "I've got nothing to give your people. Didn't you hear me? I'm broken. I can't go five minutes without crying. I lock myself up in dark rooms and hide out under blankets. I have no powerful sermons on file to yank out and redo."

"Dennis, I can't wait to see what God is going to do next week when you come," was his calm reply.

I gave him one last chance to give up on me. Heck, I told him I'd even given up on me.

He chuckled and said, "See ya soon."

I decided to go, but I told God that when this blew up in His face He shouldn't say I hadn't warned Him. I went, armed with my Bible, a blank yellow note pad, and a case of Kleenex.

One of my assignments was to speak to the church board on prayer and leadership. I was standing in front of ten folks waiting with empty paper and pens in their hands to hear from the prayer warrior. The room felt more like a prison than a church; I felt trapped with nowhere to run. I was introduced by the pastor in a very low-key way. He never promised anything; he just said, "Dennis wants to share a few things with us this week. He's been going through a tough time, but I told him to just be himself." Four out of the ten kinda clapped, pretending to be glad I was there.

I stood up feeling completely naked and ashamed. These guys have no clue how screwed up I am. Maybe I'll just fake it and go through the motions; they'll never know the difference.

Before I could say a word I sprinted to the bathroom to throw up. I locked the door, hoping to spend the next week in there, anywhere but out there with those perfect saints full of light. Seeing their light only condemned my darkness.

In the bathroom I remembered earlier walking by one of the church guys who'd been smiling and whistling. I'd been so jealous of his joy I wanted to pitch him and his happy self out the stained glass windows; I hadn't because that would not have been Christlike. I'd simply looked at him and growled.

I finally walked out of the bathroom and into the boardroom. I stood like a cardboard cut-out before them, saying nothing. They knew something was wrong but didn't know what. I gently eased out my opening statement.

"I'm not happy with God right now, and I don't think He's happy with me. I think I did something to offend him, but I'm not sure what that is. I think I've lost God's love, and I don't know how to get it back. And, oh yeah, my name's Dennis."

Trust me—that was not the best way to kick off a week of revival. I couldn't remember everything I said, but I do remember a lot of it did not make me or God look very good. I wondered why any pastor with half a brain would want some guy who wanted a divorce from God to speak to his precious flock. If I'd been the pastor of that church, I would have wrapped me in a white suit and checked me into a padded room. Even that would have been better than being trapped with a churchful of perfect people for a week.

I limped through the whole week, speaking on brokenness and darkness every night. I needed no notes. I spend as much time in the bathroom as I did behind the pulpit, maybe more. I had no PowerPoint presentation; I didn't think I had any points at all. I gave no proper conclusions or clever applications at the end of the services.

It was the last night of this train wreck of a week these nice folks had been forced to witness. I'd run out of gas and had nothing left to say. I felt they didn't want to hear one more syllable on darkness. I closed by asking people if they had anything to say about our week, good or bad. I held my breath, waiting for my forty lashes, but what happened instead was people actually said thank you.

At times I can be a real glutton for compliments, so I asked, "Thanks for what?"

One said, "Thanks for inviting us into your darkness and letting us walk a few miles together."

Another added, "You said what I have thought for years about my life, but because I'm a leader here I just fake it to make it through. Faking it keeps people away from my darkness. When they ask if I'm okay I just say, 'Yep—God is good all the time and all the time God is good' or something that sounds spiritual. Most people buy it, and I can go back and live silently in my darkness. You came here and told us up-front you're messed up. The truth is we're all messed up, but we've trained ourselves and the church to lie to protect our pain and reputations. You just showed up and vomited your hurt all over us. What's weird is that in some strange way you've given us hope this week. Yeah, it sucks being you right now, but God has used you to show our church it's okay to say we hurt and are ticked at God and not get zapped by lightning."

The clock in the back of the sanctuary told me it was time to go home; I was tired of living in a bathroom for a week with a toilet for a roommate, but as I looked out into the congregation I saw a lady dripping wet with tears, staring at me. I just looked at her, letting her know I'd wait out whatever she had to say. Once again I ended the week like I started it, by standing like a piece of cardboard and saying nothing.

She stood and spoke. "Remember last Saturday when you came and spoke to our board? I thought it was too good to be true. Here comes the right hook of fellowship."

"Yes ma'am, I'm sorry about that."

"Remember what you said to us to start the meeting? How you were messed up and living in darkness?"

"Yes I remember."

"Do you remember saying you were angry with God?"

"I remember it well, very well."

"That was what I'd been feeling for a while. My young granddaughter died; I thought I'd heard God say He would heal her. Our whole church thought God was going to heal her. Everybody thought God was going to heal her but God. Right or wrong, I am so angry with God for snatching her right out of our family's hands. The day she died is the day the darkness took my mind and soul hostage. Every day I think about her. I wish God could take me and bring her back. I so miss her I'd do anything to be with her. So this week was going to be my week to 'Do anything to be with her.' I would rather be with her than here; I am like you, trapped in the dark with no switch to be found.

"I was going to give God one more chance to lift this darkness by coming to this prayer, revival thing. I told myself and God, If this guy comes in and give us a pile of religious crap, I'm giving up. I've been to many of these spiritual pep rallies. and most end the same. We are told to pray more, read more, do more, love more, fast more and, hallelujah! God is good, amen; let's eat ice cream with sprinkles on top.

"But Dennis, you came in and just listened to our pain and let us listen to yours. You never tried to fix us; you just loved us, bumping into walls in the dark. I thought you might want to know that your darkness has helped me find the switch. Your darkness has brought so much light to our messed-up lives, my messed-up life. I've played the church game for over sixty years, but not this week, not today. This week it was either God showed up or I checked out. You know what it's like to almost take your life, don't you, Dennis?"

I didn't know if I should or could 'fess up to something so dark in a room so full of light, but "Yes, I know what it's like to want to die more than live. I know what it's like to sit in the dark, alone, feeling more lost than found."

She smiled and said, "Thanks for the light."

This is what my darkness has taught me: God uses our dark times just as much or more than our light to change the world. I'm not proud of my darkness and pray I will never, ever, have to be dragged into a dark room again anytime soon.

I'm not sure how or why it works this way, but when we share our scars with others it helps heal theirs. Maybe this is why Jesus' darkest day, the cross, has brought so much light to so many. I'm not proud of entertaining voices that encouraged me to pitch myself in front of a semi, and I'm petrified of what my family and friends are going to think of me when they read this story. What are my daughters' friends going to think of them because of me?

This is the last story I have written for this book because it took all the courage I could find to write it. For two years I've been begging God to let me slide on putting ink to my darkness. But the reason I finally wrote it was because there are people out there (maybe you) who are sitting in the dark with no switch to be found. Maybe you're sitting at a stoplight waiting for an eighteen wheeler to do what God won't. Maybe you're at a cemetery draped over a tombstone of a loved one wishing it were you down there instead them. Maybe you feel God is mad at you. Maybe you can't remember what His voice sounds like and are standing on the edge, gazing down, thinking, Maybe six feet ain't so far down.

God never promised us a life without darkness. God never promised us a life full of ice cream and sprinkles. He promised us he wouldn't leave us or forsake us.

One of the few verses that cast a flicker of light on my season of darkness (it did not last forever, but it felt like it at the time) was from the book of Job. Job is suffocating from the dense darkness that he has been forced to camp out in. For what? For being the most righteous man on the face of the earth? Boy, that sure motivates me to be good! What a bizarre reward for not crashing into the Ten Commandments ... darkness.

Job is tired of looking for a switch God has padlocked. Then, a few seconds before the eighteen wheeler comes along, he cries out from the darkness a few words that bring light to millions:

But if I go to the east, he is not there;
if I go to the west, I do not find him.

When he is at work in the north, I do not see him;
when he turns to the south, I catch no glimpse of him.
But he knows the way that I take;
when he has tested me, I will come forth as gold. (Job 23:8–10)

Job is saying, "I've gone to church, read the books, prayed, fasted, given to the poor, and still I'm bumping into walls." He did everything right but still can't find the switch! So his conclusion is, "I'm sure glad when I can't see God, God can see me."

He, like I, realized that sometimes all we can do is stand in the pitch-black darkness of our lives and let God find us. Even though we can't see Him, He can see us. Even though we have lost Him, He hasn't lost us. He is in my darkness. He is in your darkness.

This happened several years ago. I am so glad I am here versus having been run over by a truck. I would have missed so much life by taking mine. Please, please, don't jump, don't swallow, don't shoot, don't hang, don't quit ... God does love you even in the dark!

"Never will I leave you." Hebrew 13:5

Here are a few places to call for help

Website for help: http://suicidehotlines.com/michigan.html

Suicide Hotline: 1–800–SUICIDE /1–800–784–2433

TTY (hearing and speech impaired) 1–800–799–4TTY /
1–800–799–4889

Conclusion

Sometimes the longer a person is a Christian, the easier it is to be a phony. The more gold stars we collect for being good, the easier it is pretend to be good. The higher we rise in the church world, the more difficult it becomes to admit our flaws, failures, and frustrations. At times our spiritual seniority curses our ability to be real. Once some people fly to a certain altitude in the church, they feel the need to maintain their Christian "image."

This false logic says, "How dare you, Dennis, keep making the same mistakes. You have been in the church 337 years now, so you should know better." So instead of just admitting we made a mess, we pretend to know how to "pour our own ketchup." We don't want people to see our scars, just our bumper stickers because it's easier that way.

When we were brand-new believers, we messed up but didn't care who knew about it; we just said, "Hey, God, I blew it, forgive me" and we moved on as we should have. When we were new Christians we didn't need a shopping cart full of Christian paraphernalia to prove our faith and love for God. We didn't need to memorize the New Testiment to show it. Shoot, we just led with His love and our open journals.

When God invited me to write these stories I told him no. It had little to do with writing a book, as I had always wanted to do that. The real fear was that when people would inspect my journal I'd hear them say, "You mean you've been a Christian for almost thirty years and you're still tripping over the same cracks? Dennis, you should be beyond that by now."

Maybe you feel you're still stumbling over the same cracks and God is behind you yelling, *Stop tripping! You're embarrassing me!* Maybe you feel you have drifted too far to ever be looked for or loved again. There is nothing worse than being lost and thinking nobody is looking for you. Maybe guilt has kicked down your door, tossed you out of your favorite recliner, stolen the remote, and is forcing you to watch reruns of your flaws, failures, and frustrations. Maybe you, like me, think it would be easier at times to throw in the towel than fight another day. Maybe you feel your hurt has somehow disqualified you from His hope.

I get a lot of the Bible and what it means to do this or that, but one thing I don't get is His love for me. I get the wrath. I get the part that says I'm a sinner. But what confuses me at times is why God still loves me even after He has read my journal and knows the real me.

What if we have the wrong view of God? What if when God peeks in our journals He weeps over all the hurt secretly suffocating between the beige pages? What if He isn't mad at us for something we did in '87 or '55 or '03? What if He has already forgiven us and is just waiting for us to forgive ourselves? What if it's in our deepest, darkest moments that God is with us in our dark rooms, and under the blankets? Yes, there are times we all feel God has left our stories because of some foolish thing we did or didn't do. I know hurt can do its best to make a liar out of hope and God's love.

Pouring Ketchup is about four people who walked into McDonald's one day and changed my view of what it is to be real. They didn't skip in somewhere between hurt and hope. They found a way to be at both places at the same time and still giggle like they were at a junior high dance. I would swear on a stack of Bibles as high as the Empire State Building those four never would have thought they had helped me find the courage to step up to the microphone and give the world my one sentence camouflaged in thirty-nine stories. So here is what I would say to the world if I had only one sentence.

"No matter what you have done, no matter what your journal says, God still loves you!"

Thank you.

I hope some of you liked *Pouring Ketchup*, but I'm sure some of you thought *Dang, I could have bought a bucket of wings and a Coke instead*. Either way I am so grateful you took the time to sift through a few pages of my first book. I can't tell you how many late nights I have prayed for all the eyes that would someday glance at these pages. I pray you will find hope in your story as you read about others looking for it in theirs.

CPSIA information can be obtained at www.ICGtesting.com
Printed in the USA
BVOW011815041012

302177BV00002B/5/P